The Sermon for Children

A Research Handbook
for Church Leaders

By

Paul M. Adams, M.Div.; M.S.;
D. Min.

THE SERMON FOR CHILDREN

FIRST EDITION
Copyright © 1994 by
Paul M. Adams

Library of Congress Catalog Card Number: 94-73315

ISBN 1-55673-971-0   PRINTED IN U.S.A.

Dedication

To Martin E. Lundi
Bishop, Pastor, Teacher
One of the First to Recognize
the Necessity of the Sermon for Children

FOREWORD

A great contribution to the church has been made with the publication of this book. During 1994 I will enter into my fourth decade of preaching to children. Nevertheless, the insights and research of Dr. Adams, combining his expertise in education and theology, have produced many points of light for me. Anyone who shares in the responsibility of developing another person's system of values based on the gospel knows it as a formidable task. *The Sermon for Children: A Research Handbook for Church Leaders* is required reading for such a person. Once read, the reader is compelled to put into practice the principles set forth.

If you have never preached to children and are considering a preaching program to children, Dr. Adams has provided you with a great resource of practical principles which will motivate you to begin preaching to children with confidence. If you are already preaching to children, he has clarified the task, shared numerous insights, provided 329 practical sermon studies, and succeeded in motivating one toward renewed zeal to continue to improve preaching to children.

The book is a wonderful addition to the library of every person who takes seriously the plea of Jesus, "Feed my sheep!" This text should find its way into the hands of every present and potential professional church worker whose ministry will inevitably touch the lives of many children.

"WELL DONE GOOD AND FAITHFUL SERVANT"

Martin E. Lundi
Naples, Florida
Easter, 1994

TABLE OF CONTENTS

PREFACE

What has been needed in the churches since the introduction of object lessons for children over twenty years ago is a construct or a paradigm that raises the simple object lesson for children to its rightful place in the worship life of the congregation alongside the Sermon of the Day as the Sermon for Children.

Until something better appears on the scene, *The Sermon for Children: A Research Handbook for Church Leaders* attempts to be the construct that elevates sermons for children to that respected place in the worship life of the church.

Young seminary graduates and pastors and teachers often have not been prepared to deal creatively and professionally with the demands of the sermon for children. As often as not, these shepherds must rely upon the prepared material of others in order to offer object talks for children during worship services.

The publication of this research handbook on the sermon for children will enable young pastors (and older as well) and church leaders to raise confidently the object lesson for children to its rightful place as the sermon for children in any congregation they serve. The handbook will teach church leaders how to select material for the sermon for children, how to formulate necessary outlines, how to confine the sermon in length, and how to wrap the sermon for children into a formal, legitimate, and dignified position in the life of the church.

While church leaders have searched for years for a meaningful way to incorporate children into the core life of the church in a vital way, it must be understood by church leaders, clergymen, and teachers first that the little ones of Christ are just as important to the life of the church as are adults. It is the belief of this author and researcher that pastors and teachers who learn the material in this handbook on the sermon for children will have made that first necessary step in incorporating children permanently into the central core life of the church, first as children and later as adults.

This handbook for church leaders can be a seed that begins a needed revolution in Christian churches for the true incorporation of children into Christ's church.

INTRODUCTION

During the last two decades, the sermon for children has begun to play an important if irregular part in the worship life of the church. For too long children were expected to sit quietly in church and to learn the living faith through some form of theological osmosis by somehow gleaning the truth from largely incomprehensible music, words, and actions.

To put it mildly, in the middle 1970's the sermon for children stormed into the church, filling a vacuum that was needed for many years. Soon church leaders were swamped with advertisements for books of completed sermons for children, prepared normally in view of the lectionary system of the denomination. To a large extent, even today denominational publishing houses only offer to church leaders these booklets of prepared sermons for children.

What was missing then and what is missing now is a research handbook that actually trains pastors and teachers in the proper, creative construction of the sermon for children. The single most important difficulty with the sermon for children is that although it is simple and short, the sermon is difficult to prepare time after time in a fresh and exciting manner. As with other aspects of the worship service, people who hear and enjoy the sermon for children soon learn to expect top quality and are satisfied with little else. This results in more pressures on church leaders who are already being pressed for performance in many ways.

The consequence of the sermon for children being introduced into the worship life of the congregation without formally training church leaders in its use and construction has led to two results. Except in the case of unique leaders who have taught themselves, the sermon for children today is usually the work of another, or it has faded in significance and use as a regular part of the worship community.

There are numerous problems connected with using materials prepared by someone else. Often more time is expended in reworking the material of another than if the leader had started from scratch altogether. Sometimes the sermon for children comes across as dull or stinted because it is not a work of the heart, but a copy. Further, when using the work of another and needing notes and manuscript, the sermon for children becomes mired in delivery. Finally, the books published recently on the sermon for children have developed the sermon to such an extent that the sermon becomes too time consuming to use, including too many objects at a time, to a degree that the sermon for children has become nothing more than a shorter version of the sermon of the day.

The other result is that the sermon for children has been discarded by many church leaders altogether. Never having been trained at the seminary or college in the proper construction and use of the sermon for children, leaders find it a simple step to either make of the sermon a simple object lesson or to discard it completely. Leaders who are not adroit at sermon preparation in general allow the sermon for children to fall by the wayside. Others, hearing objections from parishioners when the sermon for children is not what it should be find it easier to stop buying and using the work of others.

The current need, then, is for a research handbook on the construction of the sermon for children containing numerous ideas and methods of keeping the sermon what it was originally intended to be when it was introduced into church life two decades ago: a simple, straightforward presentation of the good news using a minimum of time and objects to get the message across to children in an inspiring and life changing manner by a church leader in the main worship setting of the local church.

The following material will assist the conscientious church leader, whether ordained or lay, in planning and developing an unlimited number of original sermons for children for the growth and edification of God's little ones.

CHAPTER ONE

The Sermon for Children - A Rationale

Something demanding inclusion in the regular life of the church must have a rationale sufficient to overcome objection. Such a rationale for the sermon for children has been lacking in the past. Because of this, the sermon for children has not been elevated effectively to a permanent position in the regular worship life of the modern Christian congregation.

The sermon for children is essential in the modern church because children need, as much as adults and parents, the food of the gospel in digestible form in order to grow and be nourished in the spiritual life. If the church as servant and steward of the mysteries of God does not produce this growth and nourishment, in many cases the child may starve for lack of spiritual feeding. The provision for a regular sermon for children in most worship services of the church takes seriously the command of the risen Lord to "teach all nations," which includes children.

We cannot expect that spiritually neglected or mistreated children will someday turn into dedicated members of the Lord's church. More than likely such neglect will lead them to serve another master in maturity. On the other hand, we have every right to expect that those who are carefully nourished as children in the glory and power and reality of the gospel will indeed produce the fruits of that very gospel in their lives. The sermon for children is meant to convey to children that they are in every respect as important as adults before God and in His church. The promise of the church in baptism to nurture and to admonish the child in the knowledge of the Lord continues in a weekly manner in the form of the sermon for children. The modern church identifies the child as an equal member of the church alongside adults.

Though older members may not want to accept the fact, recent studies have revealed that there is something drastically wrong with the Sunday School programs around the nation. Though some isolated congregations are increasing Sunday School numbers, many others face the real possibility of closing the Sunday School for lack of participation. It is safe to say that changes in the American lifestyle have undermined the chances of success for the Sunday School and that there is nothing visible on the horizon to change this situation in the very near future.

With the decline of the Sunday School system comes the increased need to feed children with the living gospel when they are available. That place and time of availability now appears to be in the church service alongside parents when they do come to worship. To overlook this important aspect of modern living would be a grave error on the part of the church leadership of individual congregations. The decline of the Sunday School may be considered a tragedy by some, but the new reality must be recognized and a place made in the regular worship service for the nourishment of children on a continuing basis. Though the sermon for children alone cannot fill the void left by the decline of the Sunday School system, it can assure that regular, acceptable spiritual feeding of children be a priority in every worship service of the church.

Children need the special touch of the hand of God just as the little ones needed the special care of the Savior long ago. Jesus blessed the children then and He intends to bless them today. The children who hear the gospel words of the sermon for children understand that it is not simply the minister speaking to them, but they fully realize this is the way that God has elected to speak to them in public worship.

Today, children bring an awareness of life to the worship service that perhaps young people in more innocent times could not. The child of today is fully aware of the realities of the modern world. The modern child is completely aware of its mortality in the urban setting. The problems of joblessness, economic ruin, homelessness, crime, mortgages, credit, broken families, hopelessness, and despair are never far from the life of the modern child or its associates, friends, and relatives. This is all the more reason to provide a regular place in the worship service where the very real problems of children can be addressed honestly and effectively with the gospel. The sermon for children can touch the hurting part of life and bring healing on the wings of the gospel just as we expect the sermon for the adult to do.

Another reason for advancing a special sermon for children in the life of the church is to assure a continuing situation in the church where doctrine can be taught. Increasingly, the average person on the street is painfully unaware of the basic tenets of the Christian faith. We live in a complex society where opposing doctrine seeks to be heard. The child is exposed to doctrinal viewpoints from aggressive friends, television, so-called "non-denominational" bible studies, and so forth. The church must provide a regular time during which the child is exposed to true biblical doctrine in the sense of the clear fundamentals of Christianity.

And finally, we must be reminded of the importance of the child in the Savior's heart: "Suffer the little children to come unto me, and forbid them not, for of such is the Kingdom of God." The church must not fail in bringing the life giving message to children through many means and a sermon for children in the central worship life of the church on a regular basis is the best place to begin.

## CHAPTER TWO

The Child in the Sermon for Children

When speaking about the child in the sermon for children, the concern is about the needs of the whole individual just as the needs of the whole individual are to be met in the sermon for the adult. Every minister or teacher is aware of the difficulty in attempting to meet the needs of a large group of different adults at one time. The same difficulty pertains in addressing the multiple needs of the child.

Chronologically, the child who is the object of the sermon for children is anywhere from two years old to about twelve years old - thus the audience of a sermon for children may contain all the developmental stages of childhood lumped into a single group. The minister will have to review the developmental stages of young people in order fully to tap the resources that such stages make available. For instance, the conception of God in the four year old stage is far less complex than the picture of God the ten year old possesses. Likewise, the distinction between right and wrong is far more clear cut for the toddler than it is for the junior high student who is beginning to study politics and history in school. The minister must assess the developmental stages of the younger audience and decide to which stage the sermon is to be addressed. In preaching to the youngest stages of children in the audience, the minister can still address older children who have been through those stages before because older, more experienced youngsters will be able to understand. A familiarity with the developmental processes in childhood will assist the minister or teacher to develop understandable and cogent sermons that will meet the needs of the listener.

General learning theory is also helpful to the minister in speaking to the child in the sermon for children. Several constructs of learning and comprehension can be helpful here.

C.C. Fries understands three stages in learning:

1. Transfer Stage - the child can learn to read simply by starting with what he knows and transferring from auditory signs for the same signals.
2. Productive Stage - from imitation and practice the child can read automatically, understanding the symbols and the concepts beneath them.
3. Vivid Imagination and Realization Stage - the symbols themselves stimulate imaginative realization of vicarious experiences.

Though there are many psychological theories of learning, a general theory of learning includes three stages:

1. Manipulative - this is an action stage, involving single idea attention and has a short attention span. Sensation is more important than thinking.
2. Reflective - this involves organization where internal ideas and perceptions are related to larger chunks of external information not known before.
3. Language - the final stage is when the child considers the words themselves rather than the objects and there is a fusion of newly learned language with what he already knew.

In addition, since the minister and teacher are interested in understanding and comprehension in the sermon for children, it is important to look at some of the constructs for comprehension educators work with. Harold Herber demonstrates three levels of comprehension:

1. Literal level - just exactly what the author is saying.
2. Interpretive level - just what does the author mean be what he is saying.
3. Applicative level - how can the hearer make use of what the author says.

Additionally, George Spache, a well known reading educator, lists five steps in his understanding of comprehension:

1. Cognition - recognizing information.
2. Memory - the retention of the information.
3. Divergent production - logical and creative ideas.
4. Convergent production - draws conclusions and does inductive thinking.
5. Evaluation - includes critical thinking and judging.

Recent research on how children learn is important, referred to here as learning styles. Learning styles research has indicated in the last few years that there are three basic ways or styles that children use to learn. One style is called left brain. Another style is right brain. A third style is integrated hemispheric learning. The child who prefers the learning style of left brain is using the preferred learning style of the left hemisphere of the brain. The left side of the brain perceives differently than the right side. The left brain learner is characterized by rationality, objectivity, formality, analyzing, writing, sees cause and effect, and theorizes. The right brain learner is characterized by intuition, subjectivity, synthesizes, uses pictures rather than words, solves problems by looking for patterns and configurations, and prefers essay tests. The integrated learner can learn through both the left and right brain processes.

What is important about learning styles for the church leader who wishes to produce meaningful sermons for children is that roughly one half the student population is either left brain dominant or left brain leaning and the other half is right brain dominant or right brain leaning. What this means is that the minister must learn to employ left brain and right brain teaching strategies in order to be meeting the needs of the entire audience of children. In other words, the purely analytical must be coupled with the purely intuitive. Words must be coupled with pictures. Concrete experience must be coupled with abstract conceptualization. Teaching to one learning style only results in half the audience being left out. Teaching to both learning styles, on the other hand, insures that the message is receivable by all three types of learners. There are numerous books available on the market that prepare educators to teach to different learning styles.

The minister who is interested in producing effective sermons for young people week after week will become acquainted with the developmental stages in children, how they learn and comprehend, and anything else necessary to understand this special audience. If the minister uses nothing else from learning theory than the fact that when you start with what is already known and the idea that children are highly motivated when their learning styles are addressed properly, their learning ability will be engaged and there will be little difficulty in producing thought provoking and interesting sermons for children on a regular basis.

Now, there is another sense in which we discuss the "child" in the sermon for children. By this is meant that indescribable anticipation and attention the child innocently displays when that child knows that God is speaking directly to him or her. The eyes begin to sparkle, the head lifts up, the body becomes tense with excitement, and there is a sense of wonder about the child that something good is going to happen. We may call this readiness - an imminent receptivity to the message of the gospel, or what God has to say. This readiness is an attribute of every redeemed child of God. This readiness is contagious and when it presents itself in the worship service, the leader will find the "child" in the adult who begins to demonstrate the same readiness at the beginning of the sermon for children. Oh, if we can only perceive this readiness in God's children and speak the powerful words of the gospel to it!

The task of the pastor or teacher, therefore, is to truly understand the child for whom the sermon for children is prepared. So many untrained people miss the mark by missing the children altogether! The minister will understand learning and comprehension principles. The minister will learn to have a facility teaching to different learning styles. The one who truly understands the "child" in children will produce life changing and life strengthening sermons for little ones!

## CHAPTER THREE

The Source of the Sermon for Children

After years of personally experimenting with developing effective sermons for children, after analyzing the work of others in the worship service, and after studying the very limited published material concerning the sermon for children, the author is convinced that the source of the sermon for children is the Book of Books, the historically accepted written scriptures of the Christian church. Scripture alone contains the food with which the child of God is to be nourished and brought up in the admonition of the Lord. All other sources for the sermon for children pale in comparison to the power inherent in the written scriptures. "They are they which testify of me."

The minister who spends time dreaming up fantastic ideas for the sermon for children from the stuff of the world will soon find that fountains other than the scripture will dry up and not bring forth the waters of life.

While illustrations from the world are sometimes helpful, the real substance of the sermon must always come from the living word if the purpose of the sermon for children is to be met effectively. Fancy titles that are borrowed from the current scene in life often become the substance of the sermon instead of the illustration they were meant to be. Many such outrageous titles come to mind. "What You Always Wanted to Know About God and Were Afraid to Ask." This title will conjure up the subject of sex. "We Know What You're Looking For" will have people thinking about their credit card balance. "Quality is Job #1" brings to mind the motor industry. "Have it Your Way" will help children start to drool for fat hamburgers. "Nobody Does it Better" will have people lip-singing about the virtues of the vacuum cleaner. The strength of these titles may be apparent to some, but in reality such titles are simply gimmicks engineered to get the attention of people. Once the connection is made to a product, the helpfulness of the title disappears.

A further problem with such titles is that they are time consuming in introducing the sermon for children. Only the living word should have center stage in the sermon for children.

An example here will suffice to show the strength of scripture in a striking manner. A favorite passage of children is "Search the scriptures, for in them ye think ye have salvation. They are they which testify of me." The purpose here is to demonstrate to children the importance of bible study in finding out about the savior. The Greek term translated as search has an interesting derivation, being the term used in the ancient world for the type of tracking the hunter utilizes in tracking down his prey, which conjures up the ideas of stealth, cunning, persistence, and skill. Clearly, we are to track after the savior with the same skill that a hunter uses to track down the game! Were we to track after the savior in the scriptures, we eventually would find ourselves staring at the footprints leaving the open tomb on Easter morning...Thus the sermon for children comes from the living word, finds its illustration there, and there is slight chance that outside influences will detract attention.

What is important is that we allow the scripture, and God through the scripture, to speak. God does all things well. We cannot improve upon it. God does not require brilliance in the making of the sermon for children. He only requires us to use the brilliance that He Himself has already created. No matter how literate, how profound, or how eloquent the individual minister or teacher is, God will not ultimately bless the attributes of the minister if they in any way interfere with the message to His children. Ministers come and go, but the scripture as the source of nourishment for God's children remains until the end of time.

Those individual ministers and teachers who first faithfully search the scriptures after the savior will not lack for insightful subject matter for the child. It is a simple formula for life. We must not give the little ones the tainted meat of the world, but instead the milk of God's pure word that sustains life.

CHAPTER FOUR

The Language of the Sermon for Children

Ministers are notorious for making sermons intolerably boring through the use of words and terminology far beyond the level of comprehension of the listeners. Thus the need for a section on the language to be used with children.

The production of a manuscript is vital in producing excellent sermons for children. A manuscript acts as discipline for the minister or teacher when preparing sermons for children. Even if the manuscript is not needed in delivery, it is the manuscript that allows the minister to analyze the language to be used with children. Additionally, by means of a manuscript the actual length of the sermon can be determined.

One language need in preaching for children is to attempt as far as humanly possible to limit sentences to simple sentences or compound sentences without many dependent phrases and clauses, lest the main idea be lost in excess verbiage as in an adult sermon.

Attention must also be given to syllabication of words. As a general rule, words involving more than three syllables are very difficult for most people, including children. Excessive syllabication must be avoided in the sermon for children.

When the manuscript has been written, a word study should be conducted before the final copy is prepared. When working on the completed draft, circle all words that fall into the following categories:

1. Words with more than two syllables.
2. Words that are typical but easily misunderstood theological vocabulary.
3. Words that may be regional in nature and not known by the average child.
4. Words that are slang or common.
5. Words that relate ideas rather than concrete objects, events, or things.

Once the words have been categorized as above, the following steps will aid in correcting improper choices, in each category:

1. Is there a shorter word meaning the same thing? Use a thesaurus.
2. How might I rephrase this theological word so that I don't have to spend all my time redefining it for children? And if I must use it, do I take the time to define it simply but adequately?
3. Can I replace this regionalism with another word that is known by all?
4. The sermon is no place for slang expressions. What word can I use to replace this objectionable word? Use a dictionary of slang, then a thesaurus.
5. Is there a way to use another word that may concretize the idea better, or do I need an illustration here instead?

Another language reality to be concerned with is that most audiences remember few of the words used. The same case applies to children. Does the language of the sermon contain enough repetition that the average child will be able to repeat the theme or message in one, simple sentence?

Careful language analysis of the manuscript is necessary to assure that terms are not being used too often. Pet terms and use of words too often results in a "Here we go again!" attitude on the part of the listener.

Analysis of the manuscript will assist the minister or teacher in determining whether or not the manuscript and therefore the minister is speaking down to children. Children desire to be spoken to in language they are comfortable with. Such scrutiny of the manuscript is a theological task that crystallizes the theological dimension of the sermon. Such regular analysis also aids in the cultivation of a language that is understood and accepted by children.

A general rule for the length of the sermon should be five minutes at the most. If the message cannot be given in five minutes to children, then perhaps the message should be discarded altogether. Whether or not we approve, the child of today is geared to listening for only a few moments at a time until the next commercial interruption. The purpose is to meet the needs of the children, not those of the parents, elders, or pastor.

The discipline of preparing a manuscript, analyzing the language of the sermon, and keeping the sermon length to five minutes aids the busy minister in keeping the sermon for children from becoming too time consuming to prepare. The sermon for children that is well planned, prepared, and analyzed for proper language will result in meaningful and memorable preaching for children.

The loving minister may also consider putting together a collection of sermons for children to be given as gifts for important occasions: the rites of baptism and confirmation, the beginning or end of the school term, when children come into the congregation or when they move away. The effective sermon for children is a thing of beauty and joy and should be available for further use.

CHAPTER FIVE

The Construction of the Sermon for Children

The construction of the sermon for children follows procedures similar to that of the adult sermon or the sermon of the day. The difference is that the sermon for children is scaled down, uses a restricted vocabulary, and is less theologically complex. Inherent in the production of the sermon for young people are the same difficulties one encounters while trying to construct the sermon for adults.

A careful and cautious textual study is prerequisite to preparing an adequate sermon for children. Some individuals may feel that less is called for in directing the hearts and minds of children in spiritual matters, but this is not true. In keeping with the concept that it is the scripture alone that directs the minister when preparing the sermon for children, the exegetical process must come first. It is well known that each minister or teacher has an individual method for textual study and this must be followed prior to putting the sermon for young people into a construct.

After the exegetical process has been completed, the real task of the minister is to put what is to be said into a coherent construct, an outline from which the sermon for children is written and prepared. The homiletical task of discovering a theme and a line of direction is essential. A correctly stated theme will produce a line of direction to follow, just as water follows the river channel to the sea. Without a good line of direction, the sermon will have too many tributaries, going in endless directions that dissipate the waters of life.

The construct that is best suited for children is a proper outline. Many of the regular outlines used in the adult sermon will satisfy the requirement of finding a theme and line of direction that will result in a usable outline. Here are a few traditional outline constructs for the adult sermon that can be adapted to the sermon for children:

1. PROBLEM SOLVING
   A. The Goal
   B. The Malady
   C. The Means

2. CHRONOLOGICAL
   A. Then
   B. Now
   C. Tomorrow

3. LOGICAL
   A. If
   B. Then

4. THEOLOGICAL
   A. What God Says
   B. What the World Says About the Same Thing
   C. What the True Believer Says

5. CONVERGENT
   A. This
   B. This
   C. This
   D. All Point to This

6. DIVERGENT
   A. This
   B. Points to This
   C. Points to This
   D. Points to This

7. TEXTUAL
   A. What the Text Says
   B. What the Text Means
   C. What God Means by the Text Today

8. LINEAR
   A. Vertical Relationships Between God and You
   B. Horizontal Relationships Between You and Others

There are perhaps one hundred different outline constructs that have been used in preparing adult sermons down through the ages found in books on sermon theory and delivery. Your theological library will reveal more on the lines of those above. What is really needed are some outlines designed specifically to the needs of children who are the object of the sermon for children. Here are a few that the author has developed which will be used later in sections dealing with sermon ideas:

1. WORD STUDY
   A. One of God's Important Words
   B. What it Means in Scripture
   C. What it Means for You Today

2. GOD'S HARD SAYINGS
   A. It is Hard to Believe
   B. But, it is True
   C. So

3. DOING SERMONS
   A. God Says to...
   B. The Problem in the Doing...
   C. God's Help in the Doing...

4. THE MUSIC (HYMNOLOGICAL) SERMON
   A. The Message is Set to Music
   B. We Hear the Music
   C. We Sing God's Message

5. THE MEMORY SERMON
    A. God Wants Us to Remember
    B. We Practice What God Wants Us to Remember
    C. Now We Know What God Wants Us to Know

6. THE MYSTERY SERMON
    (Many variations can be used here)
    1. Scrambled words or sentences
    2. Flash cards that point to a solution
    3. What's in the box?

7. THE NATURE SERMON
    A. God made...
    B. He Said This Stands For...
    C. When We See This We are Reminded of God's...

8. PARENT SERMONS
    A. God Says Parents Show Love by...
    B. Sometimes it's Hard to Understand...
    C. But This is How God Wants Us to Understand...

9. THE TELEVISION SERMON
    A. What We Saw this Week
    B. What God Tells Us Through What We Saw

10. COLOR SERMONS
    A. God Uses a Color to Teach
    B. It's a Symbol (Theological Truth) for...
    C. We are Reminded of God's Love When We See...

11. GOD'S FOREVER SERMONS
    A. God Says _____ Will Remain Forever
    B. We See How _____ Exists Today
    C. We are Assured that _____ Will be Here Each Day

12. RIDDLE SERMONS
    A. Read the Text
    B. State the Question
    C. Let the Children Solve It
    D. Application

An awareness of the numerous types of outlines that can be produced for the sermon for children will produce a good variety in preaching to and for children. It is hoped that enterprising ministers and teachers will invent even more constructs for outlines for preaching to children.

Once the text and the outline have been studied, the selection of an object is necessary. Sermons that use several objects are to be discouraged because the message can easily be lost in the objects. The object should come as an integral part of the text or derived directly from it. The earnest producer of sermons for children will know well in advance what texts will be used and will be working on procuring the proper objects. Once in the desert the author found an abandoned shepherd's staff hanging on the branch of a tree. Needless to say, the staff was used for a sermon dealing with shepherding.

The purpose of the simple object in the sermon is dual: to rivet the attention of children and to keep the minister or leader on task with the theme. Children find it easier to begin with a physical object before making theological deductions and applications.

Also, while making rounds in homes or stores, the church leader will keep a good lookout for objects suitable for the sermon for children. You may use something from a parishioner's home for a sermon and then return it. The same applies for local stores or businesses. Explain your need to borrow the object for use with children in a sermon and you will not be turned down!

Directions for how the object is to be used in the sermon should be written down in the manuscript. There may be planned times where it is appropriate to put the object aside or out of sight altogether.

From start to finish the manuscript should be no longer than five minutes in complete length. Actual circumstances before the congregation usually make the sermon longer anyway.

Any questions that are to be asked of the children during the sermon should be thought out and written in the manuscript as part of the writing function in the preparation of the sermon.

A completed manuscript with proper construct, object, and directions will be more effective on a continuing basis than hastily thrown together "brilliant" presentations. The sermon for children deserves the finest theological insight and preparation that the minister or teacher can muster.

## CHAPTER SIX

The Delivery of the Sermon for Children

Personal habits and style will dictate when it comes to the delivery of the sermon for children. A normal assumption, however, is that preaching from the pulpit to children is not effective. The minister in the pulpit is much too aloof and isolated from the children for effective delivery. Also, the sermon object or illustration may not be seen by all.

There are two different methods or places from which the sermon is delivered in prominence in churches today. One method has the minister call all children forward to be seated somewhere in the chancel where the sermon is delivered. The other method is to have the minister stand at the front of the congregation and to move down into the aisle area for delivery.

The latter method is preferred, where the minister is closer to the people and can establish rapport immediately. There is little interruption to an already crowded worship time when children do not have to come to the front. Children remain seated with their parents. The sermon can be heard by all; the object is seen by all. Children can participate in the sermon even if they are too bashful to leave their seats and go forward. The entire congregation is involved from beginning to end. There is less pressure on one individual to answer questions. And often older people can assist with answering questions when children are stumped.

Since people never know what is coming next when it comes to the sermon for children, it is best to have a regular introduction and salutation formula that wraps the sermon in its context and delivery. An introduction could begin: "Good morning children. What special message does God the Father have for you today?" A salutation or blessing at the end of the sermon is also helpful: "Can you remember that, boys and girls? God bless you." These formularies immediately and clearly announce the beginning and the ending of the sermon for children. No one is confused about what is happening.

Dealing with the unpredictable response by children heightens the anticipation by all in the sermon for children. The skilled leader soon learns how to deal with the unanticipated remark during delivery. If such awkward responses have to do with the theme of the sermon, the minister may make use of them; otherwise, gently pass off such remarks with a kind word or laugh. Humor in the sermon for children can often be helpful and healthful for all.

There is no place in the sermon for children for a sermon "voice" that is not real. Children are not interested in having one more negative authority figure invading their lives. The voice should be friendly and informative and the demeanor of delivery should be one of loving concern for children. The minister is the shepherd who loves his little sheep and who is aware of their sensitivities. A normal voice for delivery allows the minister to establish a good footing with children. When the minister is comfortable in front of the people and children a similar feeling is established in the audience.

The best quality for delivery of the sermon for children is humility. The foremost quality is that the minister comes across as a fellow seeker after God's rich truths - not as an expert. The message first must have meaning for the minister and only then can it have meaning for the children. Perhaps the best term to describe the proper deportment for the minister in delivery is innocence. Children can instantly recognize whether or not an adult possesses this virtue. If you do not possess this genuine innocence, do not attempt the sermon for children on a regular basis.

Finally, in the delivery of the sermon for children there is plenty of room for the dramatic. After all, the word of God is dramatic and imbues life with meaning. The gospel is true drama. The intense moment of reflection, the awe inspiring gasp at the recognition of God's message, the sweeping of hands and arms, the shout of joy - all are useful elements of delivery in front of children. The five minutes of sermon for children is dramatic; it must be the living word.

## CHAPTER SEVEN

Introducing the Sermon for Children to the Congregation

It would be a mistake to begin using sermons for children upon an unsuspecting congregation. There will be those individuals who oppose the sermon for children under any circumstances and who are quite vocal about their opposition. At the beginning, adults and children will not understand what is expected of them in this new venture that the pastor proposes. And the first sermons for children you plan will not be the best you ever do.

A simple means of introducing the sermon for children in the congregation is to propose to the church council that to begin with the sermon for children be used occasionally, perhaps liturgically at peak periods of the church year when people expect a little more and are motivated for special celebrations. Such times would include Christmas, Ascension, Lent, Easter, Confirmation, etc. This would allow plenty of time between sermons for comments and sufficient time for planning future, effective sermons for children. Between the festivals, the minister will have an ear attuned to the general reaction in the congregation from church leaders, children, parents, and others. More than likely, the minister will be asked to include such sermons on a more regular basis.

Another method of introducing the sermon for children is to plan on having one sermon each month for one year. This will require doing the sermon for children at the best attendance Sunday of the month. The minister should announce such intentions beforehand to church leaders and to members so that they understand what is being planned and what is to be expected of the congregation. At the end of the trial period, open discussions about the usefulness and effectiveness of the sermon for children can be held.

Whatever method for introduction is used, there should be some form of evaluation of the sermon for children. This could be in the form of an inventory filled out at the end of a service in which the sermon for children was used. A brief inventory can ask pertinent questions:

1. Can you state the theme of the sermon for children in one sentence?
2. Was the length of the sermon about right?
3. Was the object useful?
4. Do you feel the message was clear and meaningful for the children?
5. About how often do you feel such sermons should be part of the worship service?

When such inventories are used in the congregation, it is important that the results are tabulated and published in the congregation so that a consensus can be formed about the validity and usefulness of the sermon for children.

Using these steps, you will soon discover that the sermon for children will be accepted as a valid part of the worship life in the congregation. The step to doing a sermon for children each week should be taken gradually lest a saturation point is reached by the pastor where the next sermon tries to outdo the one before. No one can prepare superlative sermons for children every time. Nevertheless, once the congregation accepts the sermon for children as a regular feature of the worship service, members will expect and demand excellent, meaningful sermons.

Flexibility is the key word in using the sermon for children in the congregation. If they are used weekly, it is always possible to cut back to bi-weekly or once a month. If they are used less often and there are demands for more, a new schedule can be made. There may also be certain periods during the year when the attendance of children changes. Naturally, there should be more sermons when there are more children and fewer when attendance drops off.

Once flexibility and control are lost, the minister may be in trouble. A proper conclusion would be that the sermon for children be introduced gradually into the worship life of the congregation, that scheduling be changed occasionally, and that the individual minister be in control as to when the sermons are or are not to be used.

## CHAPTER EIGHT

The Relationship Between the Sermon for Children and the Sermon for Adults

The church leader must constantly be reminded that the sermon for children is not simply a miniature sermon for adults; neither is the sermon for adults merely a larger version of the sermon for children. In many Christian churches the high point of the worship service is the Holy Communion or celebration of the sacrament. When there is no eucharistic celebration, the high point of the worship service is the sermon of the day. The next high point of the worship service should be the sermon for children.

Often the theme of the service or the theme of the sermon for children and the sermon for adults may be similar. However, the themes should never be identical or one sermon will inevitably appear to be an expansion or diminution of the other. Since the three lessons used on any given Sunday in most denominations today are related thematically, it is logical to preach one sermon from one text and another sermon from another text. This works especially well when an Old Testament theme is carried forward in the New Testament lessons for the day. The sermon for children may be, for example, a brief word study that establishes and explains the biblical concept being used while the sermon of the day may expound on the concept. The opposite approach works well also, when the New Testament lessons are used for the sermon for children and the sermon of the day expounds the original concept.

This method will produce a relationship between both sermons yet make neither unnecessary.

Another consideration should be that the sermon for children never be some isolated bit of wisdom totally separated from the theme of the service or the theme of the sermon of the day. Both should be distinct, yet related in some degree.

It is certainly proper during the sermon of the day to refer back to the sermon for children and its object for effect and interest, just as it would be natural to look forward during the sermon for children to the sermon of the day. "We want to remember this, children, because we will see more examples of this in the main sermon today." "See if you can remember what this word means when it is used later this morning." "Here the identical truth is discussed that we mentioned earlier in the sermon for children." "The object we used in the sermon for children serves as a useful illustration of this truth." "Here we have the same truth again."

In many cases the same major theme may be used in both sermons. If the sermon for the day is one that is quite profound or complicated, the use of the same text for the sermon for children will enable the worship leader to preview the difficulty with carefully chosen and understood language and object in the sermon for children before tackling the subject in the sermon for adults. Normally, when the same text is used for both sermons, it is natural to use sermon outlines that are entirely different. Likewise, the immediate or extended context may be used for one sermon and the major text for the other. This will often reduce the amount of time needed for introductory remarks or lengthy explanations.

The relationship of time between the two sermons is important, too. If excessive time is given to the sermon for children, in reality it becomes a sermon of the day. This is why the suggestion was made that the entire sermon for children not exceed five minutes in length. Under all conditions, this would leave plenty of time for the sermon of the day. As well, if the minister is used to preaching for thirty minutes each Sunday prior to beginning to use the sermon for children regularly, then it is consistent to reduce the time of the sermon for adults by five minutes.

Since in many cases when the overall theme is similar the

introductory material is covered in the sermon for children already, there is nothing to prohibit shortening the sermon of the day by a few minutes. Careful response to the reaction of the two audiences in the congregation will assist the minister here. This is another good reason for the use of sermon inventories once in a while that allow the audience to react to sermons privately on paper.

The minister will, therefore, continue to study the relationship between both sermons and determine how strong or weak the relationship should be in reference to text, theme, and time, always keeping in mind that children will come to hear the sermon for children and the adults will come to hear both sermons.

Finally, in the hectic schedule of the parish ministry, it is good practice to determine the text for both sermons and then complete the sermon for children prior to working on the sermon of the day. The discipline of reducing God's truth to a simple communicable form will always assist in preparation of the sermon of the day. In struggling to contain the message in the short time of the sermon for children, other insights that are bound to appear may be discussed at length in the sermon for the day. Both sermons are needed in the church today. Neither sermon should be neglected at the expense of either the adult audience or the audience of children.

## CHAPTER NINE

Common Problems With the Sermon for Children and How to Overcome Them

Though few ministers or church leaders are willing to admit as much, the preparation and delivery of sermons for children can be frustrating and nerve wracking. A minister was interviewed who desperately wanted to introduce the sermon for children into the worship life of the congregation, but was fearful because of the belligerent attitude of some adults who had blocked every effort the minister had made for innovation in the congregation. It is in just such a situation where the sermon for children can be effective. The effective sermon for children is an exceptional time of innocence and bonding between the pastor and children, and adults are drawn into this. The sermon for children is for children and internal bickering and squabbling between pastor and people must not allow creative efforts to deliver the gospel to children to be thwarted. The time of the sermon for children is for the church leader and the children. Adults are only involved to the extent that they happen to be present. This author has often prefaced remarks with these words: "Now children, this special message is between our Father and you. We can let the parents and adults listen, if they are good..." When we present the living gospel to children, we must be bold.

Another difficulty for some pastors and leaders is fear of being in the spotlight, especially when directly in front of the congregation at the seats or in the aisle. Many leaders are more comfortable in the pulpit area where there is distance and protection from the glare of the people. The chancel area has become a fortress where the church leader feels important and comfortable. The truth is, however, that the pastor and church leader are more in the spotlight when in the pulpit where lights are focused and loudspeakers amplify every sound. When the pastor leaves the pulpit to be out in the congregation to deliver God's saving message to the little children, the leader is now on an equal plane with the children and distance is no longer significant. When the object is used, all eyes are on the object, not on the leaders. The message and the Lord now become the focal point of attention, not the worship leader. Interactions between the pastor and children relieve any tension from the spotlight syndrome and the spotlight is now put on the essential to begin with: the living message of the living Lord to His living children. In fact, many pastors will find themselves more comfortable and relaxed in the pulpit after having first established direct rapport with the audience earlier in the sermon for children.

For some leaders, the limitations of memory become a problem when first writing and delivering the sermon for children. You recall that a manuscript was previously described as an important aspect of the preparation of the sermon for children. A well planned sermon is not easily forgotten by the minister. The outline and the object for the sermon assist here. When the worship leader is temporarily befuddled, it is a simple matter to return attention to the object of the sermon which re-focuses attention of both the audience and the minister. Another way of dealing with temporary memory loss is to ask of the children a simple question: "And, children, what do you think God is trying to say here?" Remember, repetition is a learning tool with children and there is no problem connected with repeating oneself until all becomes focused and clear again.

Another problem that interferes with the sermon for children is the unexpected comment or outburst from a child. Some church leaders dread such a circumstance as much as if the budget were not being met. Here one must keep in mind that it is precisely the unexpected that is the essence of the gospel in the first place. How many times were the disciples dumbfounded by the remarks of the Lord in his preaching? It is the truly unexpected message of the gospel that brings people back time and time again to hear the message of the Lord. Jeremiah heard the word of the Lord in the flowers of the almond branch. Moses saw the glory of the Lord in the burning bush. The old woman with the issue of blood felt the glory of the Lord in the touch of His garment. The word of the Lord may come from a child also.

The unexpected, then, instead of being a reason not to do sermons for children, can be an effective part of the sermon. The unexpected sigh of the child whose mind is suddenly penetrated by the word; the excited question of one who needs an answer right now; the response that at first glance seems preposterous but in reality is profound; the laughter that comes when we realize how petty and silly we as humans can be; the grand silence at the sound of the Master's voice - all of these unexpected and unplanned events in the sermon for children can be a vehicle for the gospel - the minister must simply have the presence of mind to accept them and use them.

Connected with this, some leaders are petrified when they think that a question during the sermon for children might go unanswered. It may be a question that no one knows the answer to at this time. It may be a question that demands a lengthy response. The responsibility in such a situation falls upon the leader. After all, the leader asked the question in the first place. Keep in mind that the rhetorical question which really needs no answer is an effective preaching tool. An effective stopping point in many sermons is an unanswered question.

Another problem for some pastors and teachers is the silence that often occurs in the sermon for children. When speaking from the pulpit, many ministers hardly take a breath in twenty to thirty minutes. When in front of the congregation to preach the sermon for children, the opposite is often the case. There is silence in getting the object before the people. There is silence when children are really thinking. These periods of silence in the sermon for children are natural elements and should not be considered a detriment but helpful in the long run. Children cannot be forced to make conclusions - time is involved and silence is essential.

How does one handle the truly off base comment or perhaps one that is totally in bad taste? These may be handled very easily by sticking with the theme of the sermon. "That may be true in another case, Johnny, but not here." "I think what you said may be important, but we will discuss it another time." "What Jesus really wants us to concentrate on here is..." "Now where was I?" Peer pressure from the rest of the congregation will soon cause such disturbances to cease.

Finally, there may be many more problems connected with putting the sermon for children into its rightful place in the worship life of the congregation. It is the belief of this author that all such problems can and must be overcome in order to elevate the sermon for children to a respectable and constant place in the worship life of the church. The real problem of the sermon for children is how to state the gospel in meaningful terms for God's little ones. When this is accomplished, all other problems become insignificant in comparison.

## CHAPTER TEN

Examples of the Sermon for Children in Final Form

At the beginning of this text, it was stated that the purpose of the author was not to write yet another book filled with prepared sermons for children. The goal is to produce a research book so that others can prepare original and uplifting and provocative sermons for children on a regular basis in the worship life of the church. Yet, the prepared sermons to follow will illustrate quite well what has been said thus far about the sermon for children. Any sermon can be improved upon, and so these could also be made better.

SERMON #1
GOD'S FREE GIFT TO YOU

Prior to the service, a beautifully wrapped gift has been placed on the altar. It is assumed that those who notice it wonder what the gift is or who is meant to get it.

Good morning boys and girls! It won't be too long now before Christmas. Yes, you'll enjoy the tree, the parties, and of course the presents. Oh, that reminds me, there is a present on the altar. Let me get it. The card reads: "To any of God's Children." I guess I'll just give it to Linda. Hold this for a minute without opening it, Linda.

As we get ready for Christmas, we are reminded of God's Word that says: For God so loved the world that He gave His only Son to die for us and whoever believes in Him shall not perish but have eternal life. Jesus, the savior, is God's gift to us. Jesus came to die and live for us in our place. That is God's gift. And what

God says is that when we open the gift of Jesus and believe in Him, then we can be assured of eternal life. We do not have to pay God back for the gift because it is the nature of a gift that it is free. When we receive a Christmas present from our parents, we do not have to pay them back for it. In the same way, God wants every boy and girl to know that God's gift of the Lord, Jesus Christ, and eternal life, is a free gift. We don't have to pay for it in any way.

Now Linda, you had no idea that you were going to receive a gift this morning, did you? No, not at all. It is a surprise, it is for you to keep, and it doesn't cost you anything. What is the only thing you can say about this? Yes, thank you. And that is how we all respond to the gift from our Father, his only Son. Can you remember that, boys and girls? That at Christmas all we need do is remember to thank God for the wonderful gift of His Son. God bless you.

SERMON #2
JESUS CAME TO TABERNACLE WITH US

Prior to the service, a small one or two man tent has been constructed and is off to the side somewhere in the chancel area so that all can see it.

Good morning boys and girls. I think you noticed something strange in the church this morning, didn't you. A tent. No, I did not sleep in there last night. I brought the tent to illustrate the children's sermon this morning. In the first chapter of the book of John, the apostle states that in the beginning or even before the beginning, the Word was with God and the Word was God, and that at a certain time the Word came to earth and dwelt among men. Now, we know that what John meant by the Word was Jesus Christ, God's only Son. He came to earth to live among men. And we also know that this Jesus died for the sins of the world and then went to live again with God.

What is important for us to understand this morning, children, is that all this was in God's plan for mankind. The text says he dwelt among us. Well, in the original Greek text the word is not dwelt, but instead it is tented. Jesus came to tent among us. Remember when the children of Israel lived in the desert they did not have a temple; they only had the tabernacle, or tent, that they took with them when they moved.

You see, a tent by its very nature is temporary. Jesus, as a man and the Son of God, came to tent with us for a while. When he had fulfilled the law and the prophets and died in our place and gave us power once again to be the children of God, his job here in a sense was completed. When it was completed he cast off the tent and returned to be with God the Father. Yes, it would be wonderful if Jesus could walk among us today, but it was not what God had planned. Just as the first tent of the Israelites was temporary, so was earthly existence of Jesus temporary. Just as the first tent of God's people was exchanged for a permanent temple in Israel, so the earthly tent of Jesus was changed for a heavenly one.

Yes, one day we shall see Jesus in His permanent and eternal being. In the meantime we are supposed to know him by the temporary tabernacle that was His when on the earth, as the loving Son of God who came to seek and to save that which was lost. Jesus did not come to live in an earthly castle; he came to live in a lowly tent until he could save us. Can you remember that, children? God bless you.

SERMON #3
YOUR SINS SHALL BE WHITE AS SNOW

Prior to the sermon a shopping bag has been placed on the floor in front of the altar. Inside the shopping bag are two shirts, one that is filthy and one that is brilliantly clean. There is also a small box of detergent in the shopping bag.

Good morning boys and girls. I hope you had a good week. I brought this bag today because the contents inside can tell us a wonderful story. Let me take out this shirt. Yuck, this thing is awful. Here's some spilled juice. There's some oil. Some dirt over here. That looks like a bit of breakfast jelly smeared on here. And here's some ink, too. I guess we can safely say that this shirt is a real mess, can't we? I think if I put this in the hamper at home with other clothes, I'd probably get in trouble, don't you think?

What can I do with this shirt? Yes, I could wash it, couldn't I? I could just throw it in the washer with some water and maybe it would come out clean, right? What else would I need? Yes, I would need to have about the strongest and best detergent in the world to fix this shirt, wouldn't I? Yes, I do have some strong detergent here in this bag. Let's pretend that the bag is the washer. I put the shirt in. I put the detergent in. After the cycle is complete, I take out the shirt and it is clean, like this one, isn't it?

Well, boys and girls, what happens with the shirt is what happens so often in our spiritual life, isn't it? We start the week off like the shirt, nice and clean. But we get up Monday morning and are angry that we have to go to school. There's a mark against us. We don't do our best work in school. There's another mark against us. Later in the week we fight with our brother and sister. Even later we don't do what our parents ask, and there's another mark. Pretty soon our spiritual lives look just like the dirty, scummy shirt! Don't they?

When such things happen to us in our spiritual life, it is important to know what God promises us. In our text this morning from the Old Testament we read of the promise of God to the people of Israel: "Though your sins be as scarlet, yet they shall be white as snow." And how were the sins of the people of Israel made white as snow? God sent His Son to be a sacrifice or cover for the sins of the people. Not only to cover the sins of the people way back then, but to cover our sins, too. Though we may in fact look much like that filthy shirt to ourselves and to others, the truth is that God now sees us as white as snow as he promised He would. Jesus has washed us of our sins, once in our baptism and daily as children of God. Yes, we may be sorry for the things we did last week, but they have been forgiven by God. This week we begin again, white as snow. Is that good news, children? Can you remember that? God bless you.

SERMON #4
YOU WILL LIVE AGAIN - AND NEVER DIE

The pastor or leader has prepared several short clippings from the newspaper that briefly itemize disasters that have happened recently. Any disasters that include children are useful, too.

Good morning boys and girls. I am glad you are here today because I have something important to remind you about. But first I want you to listen to some of these headlines I have with me from the newspaper. (Read the reports or news items at this time.) Yes, children, the world we live in is many times a very sad world. We are sad when we hear about such tragedies. Perhaps some of you have experienced tragedies closer to home. An illness. A death of a close one. Fear of some harm coming to you or to one that you love. An accident, or an illness. Yes, many times we wonder how such terrible things can happen to people.

It is at such times as these when disasters occur that we need to be reminded of some things. Jesus, too, was sad when tragedies happened in his life. The bible tells us that Jesus wept. But even in the midst of the worst tragedy He could still look at the thief on the cross and say, "Truly I say to you, today you shall be with me in paradise." For Jesus knew that the purpose of His life was to unlock the doors of heaven to all people. And he unlocked the doors of heaven to us, too. When we were baptized, we were received into God's family. And the promise of Jesus to those who are in the family of God is very clear: "He who believes and is baptized shall be saved."

So, it is not wrong that we are sad when sad things happen in the world. We cannot help but be moved by tragedies. At the same time, though, we remember that Jesus promises us life everlasting. He tells each of us: YOU WILL LIVE AGAIN - AND NEVER DIE! Even when bad things happen, we can still trust the words of Jesus: Whoever believes in me shall not die, but will have eternal life. Can you remember that, children? God bless you!

SERMON #5
THE DYNAMITE OF GOD

Prior to the service, the pastor or leader places an empty box at the foot of the altar. On the box are words such as DAN-

GER - DYNAMITE. The box is covered so that no one thinks a bomb has been planted.

Good morning boys and girls. Now I know and your parents know and you know that sometimes it is not convenient to be a child of God. Sometimes we take abuse because we believe in God and His Son Jesus Christ. Our friends might look at us in a funny way when we say we are going to church. They may poke fun at us when we say we are going to Sunday School or to confirmation class. They may call us funny names like "Bible Thumpers," or religious freaks. It can often be done in such a way that we feel embarrassed or ashamed to be Christians.

The Apostle Paul had every reason to be ashamed of the gospel of Christ. He was beaten because he believed in Jesus. He was imprisoned for his belief. He was made to look like a fool. He was stoned. He was run out of town. He was tortured because of Jesus. Finally, tradition tells us, he was killed for believing in Jesus and the forgiveness of sins. Paul had every right to be ashamed of the gospel, didn't he? Yes, he did. But you know what? He was not ashamed. He said, "I am not ashamed of the gospel of Christ for it is the power of God unto salvation to everyone who believes."

Let me uncover the box I have here. Yes, it says dynamite on it, but the box is empty. It simply serves as an illustration. The term Paul used for power is the Greek term for DYNAMITE. The gospel of Christ, Paul, said, is the dynamite of God! The gospel is the DYNAMITE that God uses in the world of spiritual matters. How is the gospel like dynamite? It is like dynamite because it has the power to change things. For this reason, some people fear the gospel as much as they fear dynamite. But we do not need to fear the dynamite of the gospel. It is the power that forgives us our sins. It is the power that enables us to know that we have the promise of eternal life. It is the power that makes our lives worth living. It is the power that enables your parents to put up with you and love you and care for you. It is the power that enables you to choose between good and bad and live a happy life. It is the power that makes your life different than the life of the person who does not know God. The gospel is the DYNAMITE of God.

How then ought we to react when someone wants to embarrass us because we believe in God and Jesus? We should simply understand that such a person does not know the power or DYNAMITE of God yet. We ought to be thankful that God has shared this DYNAMITE with us and our family. And yes, we ought to pray that God will use the gospel in some way to reach those who do not yet know Jesus. We can say with St. Paul, I AM NOT ASHAMED OF THE GOSPEL OF CHRIST BECAUSE IT IS THE POWER OF GOD UNTO SALVATION FOR ALL WHO BELIEVE. Can you remember that, children? God bless you.

## CHAPTER ELEVEN

Research for the Sermon for Children

When the church leader begins to prepare sermons for children on a regular basis, research becomes imperative. A good way to begin research for the sermon is to carry a small notebook in which to jot down ideas as they occur, often in a very spontaneous manner in doing the work of ministry. The cogent remark by an individual that may be forgotten quickly; an object that comes to mind for which a text should be found; the inspired thought that dangles in the mind for just an instant and may be lost; an experience that can be useful but must be remembered and thought about later -- all of these instances require a ready means to store the information for later use. How often do such gems of experience or inspiration become lost because they cannot be saved? Such notebook material can later be transferred to a permanent file on the personal computer for future use and development. A few notes per week become several hundred over the course of a single year and over a thousand in a decade.

Church leaders with foreign language skills and ability to work with the original Greek and Hebrew now possess extraordinary tools through computer programs that simply were not available only a few years ago. Ease of access to these materials today was unimaginable just ten years ago. Instant availability through computer programs to various concordances, translations, transliterations, word occurrences, grammatical nuances, textual variations, parsing of verbs, theological word studies and more occur through the simple manipulation of a mouse on a computer. What formerly took scholarly church leaders many hours to gather together can now be collected through computer in a matter of minutes without ever turning a single page of a book. Not only this, but completed language studies can be stored for further work in the future.

What this means for the scholarly church leader is that less time needs to be spent ascertaining what the text meant and more time can be spent on what the text means in the life of children today. More time can be invested in what is essential in the sermon for children, construction of the outline and translation of the content into the language of children today in a short, usable manuscript. Remember, the purpose of the research is to translate the scriptural truth into the easily understood language of the child.

Those church leaders who do not possess original foreign language skills can still nevertheless conduct original research for the sermon for children. The computer researcher has access to many similar tools used by scholars today. Entire translations are now available on personal computers with instant word search capabilities. Every occurrence of a word can be found in seconds. Such a list can be reduced readily to pertinent parallel passages and context. Transliterations of the Greek and Hebrew text are available where foreign terms are defined by a click of the mouse on the computer. As well, bible dictionaries, exhaustive concordances, commentaries, geographical texts, historical analyses, and theological word studies are also available in the language of the user that allow the church leader to be as close to the text in the original languages as a person can be without knowing the languages themselves. This research results in a deeper understanding of the theology of the testaments and what they originally meant.

Once the research takes place, both the scholar and the student of scriptures are on a more or less equal footing when preparing the sermon for children.

The material that follows in subsequent chapters is research available to those interested in the sermon for children and who wish to begin with a desire to spend time on the actual construction of the sermon for children. Studies on the regular lectionary series of the major denominations have been avoided purposefully so that the church leader can begin preparing sermons that are unique and not what members of congregations have already heard. Sometimes just the chapter containing the concept has been cited; in other situations the exact text is mentioned. The research for each sermon contains the following:

1. The Text
2. The Theme of the Text
3. The Major Concept of the Text
4. The Sermon Idea
5. The Sermon Outline Type
6. The Sermon Object

It is suggested that as the church leader becomes familiar with the research construct presented here, the same basic construct can be used when the individual is ready to do the research personally. Those notes discussed at the beginning of the chapter can become the basis for research on sermon themselves. Together with the 300 sermon research studies contained here and the ones developed through the personal notebook within a few years results in a treasury of 600-700 sermon ideas for children readily at hand at all times.

## CHAPTER TWELVE

The Sermon for Children From the Old Testament

The theology of the Old Testament is fully extant and developed already in the first five books commonly referred to as the Pentateuch. For those with abilities in the Hebrew language, there is little difficulty in producing objects for the sermon for children. Those with facility with Greek may use the Septuagint version of the Old Testament in producing the sermon for children. For others, biblical aids will assist in determining text and object for sermons.

Using the Old Testament for the sermon for children has not been as popular as using the New Testament has been during the last twenty years. One reason is that it is usually necessary to establish the context of the passage first to determine the historical situation of the people of Israel. This may lengthen the sermon for children somewhat. The Old Testament, however, is a rich source for the sermon for children in view of the fact that today so few children are being raised with an understanding of the covenant, characters, and prophecies of ancient Israel. Without the Sunday School and its ability to transmit the heritage of the Old Testament to children, the sermon for children can initiate this task.

Some of the most familiar stories of the Old Testament were not included in the research material. First, many of the stories are quoted in the New Testament text. Second, the Old Testament material found in the three year lectionary system used in many Christian churches contains the most familiar passages. Third, many of the more familiar passages are well suited for the longer and more detailed sermon for adults.

Much effort went into selecting passages dealing directly with the covenant and promise of redemption since these concepts have nearly been lost on the present adult population. Children at an early age can understand the Old Testament covenant and the interactions between God and His people, Israel. Often only a few verses or entire chapters were used as the basis for the sermon studies. Church leaders may key in on selected passages and texts for detailed study.

The 161 sermon studies that follow are truly representative of the literature of the Old Testament, including sections from the Pentateuch, the historical books, wisdom literature, and the prophetic books. By continuing where the author has left off and by selecting passages in the wider context of those included here, the church leader can easily produce 500-600 usable sermon studies for children from the Old Testament.

#	The Text	Theme	Major Word or Concept	Sermon Theme or Idea	Outline Type	Objects
1.	GEN 1:1-24	Creation	God said	Power of God	Chronological Theological	Examples of powerful words
2.	GEN 1:26ff	Creation of Man	Image	Created in image of God	Word Study	Mirror - the reflected image has likeness but is not the same thing.
3.	GEN 3:1-3	Sabbath	Sabbath	Sabbath is Holy	Logical	Examples of rulers setting aside special days.
4.	GEN 2:1-14	Man in Paradise	Providential Care	God's care of First People	Textual	Flash cards that show God's love by what he provided in the garden.
5.	GEN 2:15-17	Limits put on man	Good & evil	Man's place under God's care	Linear	3 boxes: one says "coke," one says "candy," one says "mystery," which would you pick?
6.	GEN 2:18-24	Loneliness	Not good that man be alone	Marriage as God's blessing	Forever	Marriage & divorce statistics - some people think they know better than God.

#	The Text	Theme	Major Word or Concept	Sermon Theme or Idea	Outline Type	Objects
7.	GEN 3:1-13	Temp-tation-Fall	Separation from God	Man separates himself when he breaks God's commands	Theological	Happy face & sad face drawn on one piece of paper, each side. The two faces of man.
8.	GEN 4:1-16	The depth of man's sin	Kill	Human life is to be sacred	Forever	Newspaper clipping showing both hate and love.
9.	GEN 5:1-32	A good generation bearing Adam's likeness	Image	Nevertheless many were righteous	Word Study	On a chart, have children pick words that would characterize people bearing the likeness of Adam.
10.	GEN 6:1-8	Wicked-ness	Favor	There are always some who find favor in God's eyes	Theological Convergent	Have children think of Scripture instances of how God shows his Love.
11.	GEN 6:1-8-7:24	The Flood	Covenant	The Covenant of Salvation	Textual	A legal contract outlining O.T. Covenant.

58

#	The Text	Theme	Major Word or Concept	Sermon Theme or Idea	Outline Type	Objects
12.	GEN 8:1- 9:28	Deliverance	Covenant	God promised seed time & harvest to end of time	Forever	A rainbow assurance of God's Love.
13.	GEN 11	Man's arrogance	Languages	Man is further separated for his sinfulness	Hard Sayings	Examples of languages. May connect to Pentecost also.
14.	GEN 15:1	God is a shield	Shield	God protects those He Loves	Memory Forever	Any object used as a shield.
15.	GEN 17	Father of Faithful	Covenant	All the faithful would call Abram Father	Textual	An example of a family tree. Abraham is our father too. We keep the covenant too.
16.	GEN 22	Test of Faith	Blessing	Through Abraham's faithfulness we have blessings today	Riddle	Jesus was part of the seed of Abraham.

59

#	The Text	Theme	Major Word or Concept	Sermon Theme or Idea	Outline Type	Objects
17.	GEN 28	Covenant transfer-red to Isaac	The Ladder in the Dream	The promise carried forward	Riddle	The ladder is a symbol of communication between earth and heaven.
18.	GEN 35	God's promise to Israel	Covenant	Kings did come from Israel	Logical	A crown symbolizing Christ or King of Kings.
19.	GEN 38-50	The story of Joseph	God carries forward the covenant blessing despite interference	God continues to come through with His promises despite interference	Divergent	A baptismal certificate shows us God addresses blessings to us today in the same way.
20.	GEN 49	Israel promises blessings	The prophesy about Simon	Jesus is that Rock of Israel	Music Sermon	The hymn, "Rock of Ages"

#	The Text	Theme	Major Word or Concept	Sermon Theme or Idea	Outline Type	Objects
21.	EX 2:1-10	The Covenant continues	God's protection of the child Moses	God's plan cannot be interfered with	Hard Sayings	A knife; illustration of the slaughter of the innocents at Bethlehem. Or, a basket as a symbol of the Ark of the Covenant.
22.	EX 4	God commissions Moses	Spokesmanship	God speaks to us today through spokesmen	Parent	Parents, teachers, pastors.
23.	EX 7-12	God is victorious over evil	Plagues	God overcomes evil in special ways	Theological	A slight poison that can be neutralized by water.
24.	EX 12	God spares the righteous	Passover	The Passover is a sign of God's mercy	Word Study Chronological	Some of the elements used in the passover meal.
25.	EX 12	Sacrifice	Lamb without blemish	Jesus was the great sacrifice	Mystery	Lamb as a symbol of innocence.

#	The Text	Theme	Major Word or Concept	Sermon Theme or Idea	Outline Type	Objects
26.	EX 14	Deliverance at Red Sea	Deliverance; saved	The Lord still delivers today	Mystery	Examples of deliverance.
27.	EX 15	Deliverance	Salvation	God's people respond to him in singing	Music	Any hymn that refers to the crossing of the Red Sea or deliverance from Egypt.
28.	EX 16	Provision	Manna "What is it"?	God can provide under difficult circumstances	Logical	Concrete examples of how God provides for our needs today. Seeds.
29.	EX 17	Grumble against God	Murmuring	We often murmur & grumble against God	Problem Solving Television	Tape recorded examples of children grumbling.
30.	EX 18	Economy of talents	Division of labor	God desires spiritual work to be shared	Doing	Organizational chart of congregation.

#	The Text	Theme	Major Word or Concept	Sermon Theme or Idea	Outline Type	Objects
31.	EX 19-20	10 Command-ments	Obedience	God tells us what we can & cannot do to be happy	Doing	Stop and Go signs
32.	EX 25	Ark of Covenant	Mercy	God's desire is to show mercy	Forever	Find chair suitable as mercy seat that covers the law (Bible).
33.	EX30: 11-16	Atone-ment	Ransom	Ransom is a picture of how God would forgive in Jesus	Word Study	Reward poster; Bag of money.
34.	EX33: 1-33	Forgive-ness	Forgiveness	Even when we break the covenant, God will forgive	Hard Saying	Something broken that can be restored.
35.	EX35: 1-30	Steward-ship	Offerings	Our offerings show our response to God's covenant	Doing	Offering envelopes, other examples.

#	The Text	Theme	Major Word or Concept	Sermon Theme or Idea	Outline Type	Objects
36.	EX 40	Presence of God	Glory of God	God often revealed His presence in special ways	Logical	Pictures of people or events where God reveals presence today.
37.	LEV 6: 1-8	Forgive-ness	Burnt offerings	Today there is one offering for sin	Theological Music	The Cross as the ultimate symbol of sin offering "In the Cross of Christ I Glory."
38.	LEV 16-19	The Great Day of Atone-ment	Cleansing	Christ atoned once and for all	Problem Solving Theological	Filter to filter out transgression. God sees us thru the filter of His Son.
39.	LEV 25	Year of Jubilee	Inheritance assured	The Joy of Redemption	Word Study Textual	Communion ware. Each Lord's Day reminds us of the Day of Jubilation.
40.	DEU 4	God is just	Some things are forbidden	Unbelief brings rewards	Hard Saying Linear	Concrete examples of results of sin.
41.	DEU 4:30-31	Return to Covenant	Repentance	Anyone may return to God	Theological	U-Turn sign.

#	The Text	Theme	Major Word or Concept	Sermon Theme or Idea	Outline Type	Objects
42.	DEU 11	Teaching God's Word	To children	Parents are to teach us the things of God	Parent	Sunday school materials, memory work, Bible
43.	DEU 28	Blessings for obedience Curses for obedience	Blessings & curses	Blessings of Obedience	Forever	A sworn statement
44.	JOSH 1:1-9	The way	Prosperity	Success as a child of God	Mystery	A map with many possible routes. God blesses the way.
45.	JOSH 4:1-7	God's Mighty Acts	Remember	We should remember & tell God's wonderful deeds in our lives	Riddle	A pile of 12 stones.

#	The Text	Theme	Major Word or Concept	Sermon Theme or Idea	Outline Type	Objects
46.	JOSH 6	Capture of Jericho	God's promise fulfilled	God fulfills promises today	Logical	Rainbow as remembrance of God's promises.
47.	JUD 14-19	Samson, man of God	Samson	A person is strongest when he depends on God	Hard Saying	Use church building & construction as example.
48.	RUTH 1-4	Meek shall inherit the earth	Meekness, trust	Small people are big in God's eyes	Theological	Examples of meek people being God's favored instruments.
49.	I SAM 3	The faithful wait upon the Lord	"Here Am I"	Readiness to serve	Theological	2 charts describing 2 models of leadership, Lord & servant types, which is Godly?
50.	I SAM 17	David & Goliath	Great and Small	God chooses the lowly to show forth his power	Forever Textual	Any type of container to show believer as a vessel of God.

#	The Text	Theme	Major Word or Concept	Sermon Theme or Idea	Outline Type	Objects
51.	II SAM 7	Prophecy of King of Israel	Offspring	God fulfills his promises	Logical	See #46
52.	II SAM 11-12	David's sin	Unfaithful to God - repentance	Great men of faith may fall yet be forgiven	Chronological Logical	Tears as sign of repentance, as with Peter.
53.	I Kings 3	Divine Wisdom greatest treasure	Wisdom	Understanding of God greater than riches	Hard Saying	2 boxes - one containing $100 bill; the other containing God's word. Which would you choose?
54.	I Kings 2	Apostasy of Solomon	Unbelief	See #52	Hard Saying Logical	See #52
55.	I Kings 19	Where is God found?	Small, still voice	God reveals Himself in strange ways	Textual	Compare outrageous & simple object to show susceptibility to the spectacular.

#	The Text	Theme	Major Word or Concept	Sermon Theme or Idea	Outline Type	Objects
56.	2 Kings 2	Power of God	Chariot of Fire	God has control over all	Logical	A globe of the earth. God upholds it in its course by His word.
57.	2 Kings 4:32-8 20:20-1	Power over death	Resurrection	God can bring the dead back to life	Word Study	A picture of the empty tomb describes this. Also the butterfly.
58.	2 Kings 20:1-4	God answers the prayers of the righteous	Hezekiah prayed	How immediate God's response can be	Forever	Telephone line might be busy. We have direct line to God always.
59.	Job 19	Confess	Witness of Believer	Testimony of faith important for others	Doing	The Order of Confession: informal confession.
60.	Job 38:9	The greatness of God	Words Without Knowledge	The smallness of man before God	Mystery Riddle Nature	Any concrete ideas that show God's wisdom; migration of birds, fish, etc..

#	The Text	Theme	Major Word or Concept	Sermon Theme or Idea	Outline Type	Objects
61.	Psalm 1	Blessed is the righteous man	Yielding fruit	Compare righteous & wicked	Nature	Small fruit bearing tree & one that is dying.
62.	Psalm 2	The king is victorious over all evildoers	Possession	God breaks the evildoers	Textual	A pot that can be broken easily
63.	Psalm 3	Putting trust in the Lord	Trust	Even in severe distress, the believer trusts the Lord	Nature	A picture of a nest of birds content and safe in a storm.
64.	Psalm 5	Covering	Shield	The believer is protected	Nature	Use the concept of a force field here.

69

#	The Text	Theme	Major Word or Concept	Sermon Theme or Idea	Outline Type	Objects
65.	Psalm 8	The eminent place of man	Dominion	Our undeserved but eminent place in creation	Theological	Objects that separate men from the rest of creation.
66.	Psalm 19	Creation speaks of God's deeds	Witness of creation	Creation glorifies God	Nature	Any created object that bears the signature of God.
67.	Psalm 23	Shepherding	Shepherd	The Lord is the shepherd	Nature	Fashion a shepherd's crook from a limb.
68.	Psalm 27	The Lord is Light	Light	We do not fear when we are in the light	Nature Logical	Darkness & Light.
69.	Psalm 31	Life in God's Hands	Time	Length of life in God's hands	Nature Chronological	A clock set to alarm, but no one knows when.

70

#	The Text	Theme	Major Word or Concept	Sermon Theme or Idea	Outline Type	Objects
70.	Psalm 32	Forgive-ness	Hiding place	When we sin God is our hiding place	Convergent	Different places we try to hide from evil.
71.	Psalm 34	Praise of God	Praise	We praise with our mouths	Music	A hymn of praise.
72.	Psalm 37	Righteous & wicked compared	Do good, trust the Lord	Do not fear the wicked	Nature	Smoke that disappears. Grass that has withered.
73.	Psalm 42	Thirst after God's word	Spiritual thirst	Spiritual thirst	Nature	2 glasses of water, one with salt mixed in - which will God give to the thirsty?
74.	Psalm 46	God is safety	Fortress	God is help in time of danger	Textual	Use example of force field.
75.	Psalm 48	God is a guide	Guide	God is your guide	Nature	A map of some treacherous terrain & the fact that you need a guide to get through safely.

#	The Text	Theme	Major Word or Concept	Sermon Theme or Idea	Outline Type	Objects
76.	Psalm 51	Forgive-ness	Mercy Repentance	How we receive forgiveness	Theological	Chart the steps in David's repentance and forgiveness.
77.	Psalm 52	Joy of the Righteous	Olive Tree	Righteous man is abundant	Nature	Tell the story of the olive tree which "seems" to outlive all others.
78.	Psalm 78	History of Israel	God's long-suffering	God never rejects his people	Hard Saying	Concrete examples where the world doesn't give second chances but God does.
79.	Psalm 84	God gives Richly	Abundance for the upright	God gives us good things	Doing Theological	Concrete examples of the good things given to the upright.
80.	Psalm 90	God's dwelling place	Richness of the presence of God	A dwelling place that is eternal	Theological	Examples of different types of houses or enjoyable things that soon decay.
81.	Psalm 91	God is protection	Shadow of the Almighty	Living in the shadow of God	Nature	Picture of eagles and their eagles.

# The Text	Theme	Major Word or Concept	Sermon Theme or Idea	Outline Type	Objects
82. Psalm 91	Clinging to God	Clinging	God's promise when we cling to Him	Problem Solving	Examples of pictures of animals clinging to their parents.
83. Psalm 95	Hymn of Praise	Worship the Lord	Singing is an act of worship	Hymn	This Psalm has been set to music, sing it.
84. Psalm 103	Divine Pity	Pity	God has pity upon us	Word Study	Examples of fatherly pity. God is the same.
85. Psalm 107	Thanks-giving	Giving thanks	We thank God	Memory	Commit v.1 to memory.
86. Psalm 118	see #85	see #85	see #85	see #85	see #85
87. Psalm 119	Harvest of the Word	The Word	Hiding the word in the heart	Memory	Different specialized vocabularies that are learned by professionals. The Believer stores words too.

73

#	The Text	Theme	Major Word or Concept	Sermon Theme or Idea	Outline Type	Objects
88.	Psalm 122	God's House	Going to God's House	Let us go to the House of God	Doing	Examples of how we find joy there.
89.	Psalm 139	God's Presence	Spirit everywhere	You cannot hide from God	Nature	Use the hide and go seek game; or atoms are everywhere.
90.	Psalm 145	God's Greatness	Unsearchable	God's greatness is unlimited	Mystery	A diamond; there are countless faces or facets that reveal their beauties in the light; or a box labeled "God."
91.	PROV. 1:7	Respect of God	Knowledge	Fear of God is the beginning of knowledge	Riddle	Flash cards with words "Love", "Money" "Car", and "Wisdom". Which is more important?
92.	PROV. 3:15ff	Wisdom	Wisdom	Wisdom makes life better	Nature	A tree; hang words on a tree like fruit.
93.	Eccl. 3:1-9	Proper season	Under the sun	Life is full of seasons	Nature	Different seasons of life pictured.

#	The Text	Theme	Major Word or Concept	Sermon Theme or Idea	Outline Type	Objects
94.	Eccl. 12	Death	Death	Seek God while ye may	Doing	Obituary column showing that young and old die.
95.	Eccl. 12:13-14	Man's duty	Duty	Our duty in life	Linear	A job description; God has given us one too.
96.	IS. 1:3	Loyalty to Master	Know	People often forget God	Nature	Concrete examples of how animals love their masters.
97.	IS. 1:18	Forgive-ness	Red & White	God forgives totally	Color	Use two pieces of cloth with same stain. Show how often it has been bleached.
98.	IS. 7:14	A child called God	Immanuel "God is with us"	How close is God?	Riddle Word Study	Shadow; although not always seen is always with us.
99.	IS. 9:6	The given Son	God's Son	The Savior's last name	Riddle	String together as one word all the titles & let children decipher his last name.

#	The Text	Theme	Major Word or Concept	Sermon Theme or Idea	Outline Type	Objects
100.	IS. 26:7ff	The smooth path of the righteous	Level Path	Different paths of life	Mystery	Compare different paths in the city; show how life is this way.
101.	IS. 40:29ff	Strength to the weak	Strength like eagles	You can soar like an eagle	Nature	Picture of an eagle in flight.
102.	IS. 44	Sin is forgiven	Israel forgiven	Sins are forgiven	Nature	Picture showing clouds one minute, gone the next.
103.	IS.45	Arguing with God	Striving with God	We are not to question God	Textual	Any craft item made by hand.
104.	IS. 49	Israel as witness	Light	A light to the nations	Theological	Flashlight with and without batteries.

#	The Text	Theme	Major Word or Concept	Sermon Theme or Idea	Outline Type	Objects
105.	IS. 54	Covenant cannot be destroyed	Covenant of Peace	Peace from the Lord	Music	Modern hymn "Shalom".
106.	IS. 55	The Word accomplishes	The Word	God's word does not come back empty	Nature	Plants in different stages of development. People are like this.
107.	IS. 56	Marker for Believer	Monument	A monument for you!	Doing	Picture of prominent local monument or model of one of national importance.
108.	IS. 57	Refuge in the Lord	Deliverance	Putting confidence in God	Problem Solving	A collection of items in which children have great confidence.
109.	IS. 60	Epiphany of Sun	Epiphany Light	The appearance of the Savior	Nature	Picture of the sun. Use this to show work of the Savior.
110.	IS. 61	Anointed Savior	Anointed	The authority of Savior	Forever	A crown, oil for anointing.

#	The Text	Theme	Major Word or Concept	Sermon Theme or Idea	Outline Type	Objects
111.	IS. 61:1	Liberty to captives	Liberty	The Savior proclaims liberty	Word Study	A model of a jail, or description of what it like to get out of one.
112.	IS. 64	Honor is a gift of God	Honor	Attempts at self-righteousness always fail	Nature	A withered leaf; a bunch of rags.
113.	JER 2:13	Forsaking God	Broken cisterns	Those who forsake God	Logical	A water pitcher that looks exquisite, but has a slow leak!
114.	JER 3	Fickleness of Israel	Harlotry	Israel was like a loose woman	Theological	Many gaudy trinkets a loose woman may use to appeal to men.
115.	JER 4	Vain attempts to beautify	Desolate one	Unrepentant sin cannot be covered	Problem Solving	Different make-up items.

#	The Text	Theme	Major Word or Concept	Sermon Theme or Idea	Outline Type	Objects
116.	JER 6:9ff	Wrath against wicked	Wrath	When God is angry	Convergent Divergent	A container of water that is slowly being filled to overflowing!
117.	JER 9	Purifying of Israel	Refining	The sinner must be purified	Nature	Any object before & after chemical refinement.
118.	JER 10	Idols are useless	Idol	Idolatry does not work	Logical	A miniature scarecrow.
119.	JER 18	Israel to be re-fashioned	Clay	The Believer is like clay	Theological	Playdough molded into a form; re-shape to show deformities; reshape again to first form.
120.	JER 23	Messiah	Righteous branch	The Savior is the righteous branch	Textual	A branch; use the concept of grafting.
121.	JER 24	Faithful Remnant	Remnant	Blessings and curses	Nature	Good and bad fruit separated.

#	The Text	Theme	Major Word or Concept	Sermon Theme or Idea	Outline Type	Objects
122.	JER 31	New Covenant	Covenant	New Covenant written on the heart	Problem Solving	Prepare a contract written on stone; another written on a heart; or something written on stone - cornerstone.
123.	JER 36	God protects his Word	Scroll	No one can destroy the Word	Forever	An original document that can be torn up; have a copy available.
124.	LAM 3:43	When God seems far away	Wrapped up	God can seem far away	Linear	Any object that portrays God being wrapped in something seemingly impenetrable.
125.	LAM 5	Result of breaking Covenant	Covenant	What people who break Covenant are like	Textual	A pair of glasses so thick that everything is distorted.
126.	EZ 3	Eating the Word of God	Word	God's Word tastes good	Doing	Different foods with different tastes; bitter and sweet.

#	The Text	Theme	Major Word or Concept	Sermon Theme or Idea	Outline Type	Objects
127.	EZ 12	The horror of exile from God	Exile	God rebukes His people	Hard Saying	A packed piece of luggage to show extended travel.
128.	EZ 13	Sentence upon Israel	Wall	God's people are rebuked	Logical	A wall of bricks that can be broken down.
129.	EZ 15	Greatness of God's love for Israel	Plighting Troth	God's love for Israel	Forever	Marriage Certificate
130.	EZ 19	Israel loses its lofty position	Scepter	Scepter removed from Israel	Problem Solving	A rod or staff resembling a scepter.
131.	EZ 20	Israel judged	Judging	God measures His people	Theological	Scales or balances.

#	The Text	Theme	Major Word or Concept	Sermon Theme or Idea	Outline Type	Objects
132.	EZ 34	God will be the Shepherd	Shepherding	God is the true Shepherd	Nature	Shepherd's staff or crook
133.	EZ 36	New Israel	Heart	Hardness of heart	Nature	Heart of stone and one that is soft.
134.	EZ 37	Valley of Dried Bones	Bones	God's Power to energize, resurrect	Nature	Any type of animal bones.
135.	DAN 12	Book of Life	Books	The Book of Life	Word Study	A huge official book or register.
136.	Hosea 11	Israel does not hear the voice	Calling	God is always calling to us	Problem Solving	Unopened letters; messages unread; invitations unaccepted.

#	The Text	Theme	Major Word or Concept	Sermon Theme or Idea	Outline Type	Objects
137.	HOS 14	Believer is like a garden	Garden	God is like a gardener	Nature	Tools used in gardening.
138.	Joel 1	Sound the alarm	Warning	God answers His people	Chronological	A portable air horn that makes a loud noise; alarm clock.
139.	Joel 3	Harvest sickle	Harvest	God shall harvest His people	Chronological	A hand sickle.
140.	Amos 4	Seek the Lord & live	Seeking	If you seek nothing, you find nothing	Problem Solving	Something hidden you have to find.
141.	Amos 8	Famine of the Word	The Word not to be found	Life when Word scarce; when abundant	Problem Solving	Something hidden you can't find.
142.	OBAD 1	Prideful shot down like eagle	Lofty Overthrown	God shoots down the haughty	Nature	Bow & arrow; shotgun.

#	The Text	Theme	Major Word or Concept	Sermon Theme or Idea	Outline Type	Objects
143.	OBAD	Wicked shall be consumed	Fire	Judgement on the wicked	Nature	Basket of dried stubble.
144.	Jonah 1	Fleeing from God	Flight	Fear of God's commands	Problem Solving	A big map that shows the flight of Jonah.
145.	Jonah 4	The Lord pities religiously ignorant	Pity upon people	The Lord wants His people to return	Logical	A pet, plant or project someone cares about.
146.	Micah 3	Rulers should be just	Oppression	Responsibility of those in power	Logical	Examples of an unjust ruler.
147.	Micah 4	Prophecy of the Remnant	Remnant	What God does with leftovers	Hard Saying	Pieces of remnants & a finished quilt.

#	The Text	Theme	Major Word or Concept	Sermon Theme or Idea	Outline Type	Objects
148.	Micah 5	Messiah to come from Beth.	Messiah	God uses the insignificant	Nature	Use example of a small community in your state; geography.
149.	Micah 6	What God requires	Requirement	What God requires	Hard Saying	Objects that could be offerings compared with justice, goodness.
150.	Micah 7	Forgive-ness	Steadfast Love	God will forget your sin	Logical	Show how easily we forget things we want to forget. How much more will God forget what he wants to forget?
151.	Nahum 3	Wicked will be destroyed	Emptiness	The wicked will be overthrown	Hard Saying	A tumbler of water that can be drained.

#	The Text	Theme	Major Word or Concept	Sermon Theme or Idea	Outline Type	Objects
152.	Hab 2	Spread the News	Vision of coming salvation	God's plan of redemption	Mystery	Use the example of popular billboards in your town.
153.	Hab 3	The joy of clinging to the Lord	Joy in the Lord	We are happy when we cling to the Lord	Nature	Habakkuk's name means clinging. Use example of child who "clings" to mother.
154.	Zeph 1	Sweeping away	Day of Judgement	The wicked will be scattered	Textual	A broom.
155.	Zeph 2	Wait upon the Lord	Waiting	God is worth waiting for	Memory	Example of anxiety while waiting for something wonderful.
156.	Hag 1	God's house comes first	House of God	God must come first	Textual	Pictures of objects that have transitory value and a picture of a church.

#	The Text	Theme	Major Word or Concept	Sermon Theme or Idea	Outline Type	Objects
157.	Hag 2	God will save Israel	Signet Ring	God will rebuild His chosen	Chronological	A beautiful signet ring to show off.
158.	Zech 3	Forgive-ness	Joshua in dirty rags	Israel shall be cleansed	Chronological	2 shirts or pants of same make; one filthy, one clean.
159.	Zech 7	The new Temple of the Lord	Messianic Temple	You are helping to build the Temple	Theological	A construction project all would like to help build.
160.	Zech 9	The humble Messiah	Humility	The Savior is humble	Hard Saying	Contrast the kinds of vehicles rulers use today.
161.	Mal 4	Sun of Honor	Messiah	Healing by the Sun of Honor	Nature	Use example of joy of basking in warm sun.

## CHAPTER THIRTEEN

The Sermon for Children From the Book of Acts

The Acts of the Apostles, or more rightly, the Acts of the Holy Spirit, is perhaps the most infrequently used text in the New Testament in the worship life of major denominations today. In the liturgical text series, one may find brief passages dealing with Pentecost or the Ascension, but little else used from this book.

There is good reason, however, for the rediscovery of this book by church leaders. The book is a graphic picture of what the church must be in order to carry out the great commission of the risen Lord. From beginning to end, the book of Acts is a tremendous proclamation of what can be accomplished in the local church if the message of the Lord is taken seriously and acted upon. Not only this, but the book portrays the type of people necessary to accomplish the mission of the church. Battling evil every step of the way, the early church found it necessary time and again to exclude some from the fellowship so that the proclamation of the gospel would not be hindered. There was no room in the fellowship for Ananias and Sapphira. There was no room for leaders who lorded it over the common person. Those who were puffed up with piety and work righteousness were excluded from the local congregation.

One wonders how modern adults could have a true understanding of the realities of the task the church faces without familiarity with the book of Acts. Many of the current problems faced by local congregations can be traced to the pathetic ignorance of what the church should be as described in the Acts.

It is the belief of the author that children must be taught the realities of church life from the beginning, from the book that best describes how churches deal with difficulty in the mission of God. In the past an idealized picture of the church has been developed in childhood and carried into adulthood that really works against the picture of church life described in the book of Acts. The reality of the spread of the Word of the Lord in Acts is epic in comparison to the average conception of church life today.

Some of the truths described in the book of Acts are readily understood by children but difficult for adults to comprehend. The Lord clearly desires and intends that His church grow. When the church is not growing, something is wrong, not with God's plan, but with people who interfere, misunderstand, neglect, or do not take seriously what God says. God often expands His church by division. He can increase it by subtraction. The power of the gospel is sometimes strongest in the weakest of situations. God takes the weak and makes them strong. The hand of the Lord can do anything. That which looks good and pure can often be evil and impure. No situation is so impossible that the power of God cannot prevail. The concepts are easily understood by children.

One of the best ways to approach the book of Acts is to ask a simple question at every turn of the text: HOW DOES THE HOLY SPIRIT? The answer to this question is the same today as it was nearly 2,000 years ago! If only our children were taught what the church really is and could carry this belief into adulthood as members of local congregations.

#	The Text	Theme	Major Word or Concept	Sermon Theme or Idea	Outline Type	Objects
162.	Acts 1:6-11	Restoring the Kingdom	Kingdom	Only God knows the time; we are to be witnesses in the meantime	Mystery	A large clock with a red second hand.
163.	Acts 1:12-14	Fellow-ship	Prayer	Early church was a close community	Doing	One loaf of bread as sign of fellowship; see also Acts 2:42.
164.	Acts 1:15-26	Offices in the church	Ministry	God directs the ministry in the church	Logical	Casting lots; votes.
165.	Acts 2:1-4	Universal Gospel	Tongues of fire	Good news is for all men	Forever	Use JN 3:16 in many languages to show need of ministers blessed with language ability.
166.	Acts 2:37	Salvation	How	How people are forgiven; repentance and baptism	Word Study	Use Baptismal font to explain repentance and forgiveness.

#	The Text	Theme	Major Word or Concept	Sermon Theme or Idea	Outline Type	Objects
167.	Acts 2:42-47	Growing church	Adding	God truly desires to add to His Church	Problem Solving	Use a bucket containing large beans to explain local church growth or lack of it.
168.	Acts 3:1-10	Healing of lame man	Amazement	The miraculous is used by God to draw attention to the Gospel	Convergent	Examples where people have turned to God after a similar miracle.
169.	Acts 3:16-26	Covenant open to all	Covenant	Covenant is inclusive	Theological	Example of exclusive clubs, organizations which limit membership; the church does not.
170.	Acts 4:1-20	Knowing the Lord brings boldness	Boldness, courage	Have we been with Jesus?	Divergent	Demonstration of why boldness is needed in believers.
171.	Acts 5:1-11	Judge-ment	Deceit in the church	The church is no place for treacherous people	Hard Sayings	Examples where people are removed from church.

#	The Text	Theme	Major Word or Concept	Sermon Theme or Idea	Outline Type	Objects
172.	Acts 5:12-16	The special honor due the Apostles	Apostles	The works of the Apostles were in fact unique	Textual	This text is a clear reason why just anyone cannot perform miracles. Ask one of the children to change a glass of water into wine.
173.	Acts 5:17-40	Leaders oppose the Gospel	Opposition	There will always be opposition to the church	Forever	Recent examples of opposition to the church.
174.	Acts 11:1-19	Divisions solved by Word of God	Criticism	Conflict in church solved by Word	Doing	Examples that demonstrate the supreme position of "Thus Says The Lord" in the church.
175.	Acts 11:26	Believers are derided	Christian	God turns even a derisive term to good use	Logical	Discuss the term "Christianos" which means Little Christ.

#	The Text	Theme	Major Word or Concept	Sermon Theme or Idea	Outline Type	Objects
176.	Acts 12	Deliverance of Peter	Angel	Even Herod not as powerful as God	Convergent	Examples of things only God can do.
177.	Acts 13	Sermon at Antioch	Preaching	Preaching is a means by which people come to God	Problem Solving	Have several adults prepared to tell how they came to faith.
178.	Acts 14: 19-28	Believers need to be strengthened	Tribulation	Tribulation is normal in the church	Linear	Tribulation here means pressures. Show how pressures can be strong & the need of releasing the pressures, like a valve.
179.	Acts 15	Church councils are important	Council	Many problems of growth require much of council	Problem Solving	Examples where mutual counselling is necessary. Demonstrate brotherhood of church.
180.	Acts 16:18	Paul's second mission journey	Preaching	The task of the Church is to go and preach	Doing	Big map that shows churches started by Paul. God blessed this going.

#	The Text	Theme	Major Word or Concept	Sermon Theme or Idea	Outline Type	Objects
181.	Acts 6:1-7	Division of labor	Meeting needs	The work in the Church is to be shared	Hard Saying	A long list of the many duties in the church that are done by many.
182.	Acts 8:1-8	Scattering enables church growth	Scattering	God makes persecution of church helpful	Riddle	Seeds that can be scattered to show spread of church.
183.	Acts 8:8-24	The Gospel in Samaria	Samaritan	Gospel heals even ancient wounds	Linear	A concise history of the hatred between Jews and Samaritans.
184.	Acts 8:25-40	The Good News is for all men	Ethiopian	God wants all to be saved	Color	Different color construction paper to represent races.
185.	Acts 9	Calling of Paul	Conversion	The power of the Gospel to change the heart	Theological	Discussion of the 2 names: Saul and Paul.

#	The Text	Theme	Major Word or Concept	Sermon Theme or Idea	Outline Type	Objects
186.	Acts 9:26-31	The Lord wants His church to grow	Growth	God intends his church to grow	Convergent	A plant and the many factors necessary for growth.
187.	Acts 10:34-43	Gospel is universal	Everyone	God is not partial	Divergent	Use a filter to show that God wants to see all through the filter of his Son.
188.	Acts 10:44-48	Baptism for washing	Washing	Baptism is sign of Covenant	Logical	Take something dirty and work it in water.
189.	Acts 19	Attempts to use miracles for selfish purposes	Power	The Power of God reserved for those commissioned to use it	Hard Saying	Term for miracle here is "dunamis," God's dynamite. Show what it can do.

#	The Text	Theme	Major Word or Concept	Sermon Theme or Idea	Outline Type	Objects
190.	Acts 24-41	Evil doers don't want church to interfere with worldly gain	Idols	The world doesn't want to be bothered by church	Theological	Examples where church interferes with world and resulting difficulties.
191.	Acts 20	Paul's farewell to Ephesians	Whole counsel	Duty is to preach the whole counsel of God	Textual	1 complete bible, 1 that is cut into convenient parts with hard counsel left out.
192.	Acts 21	Christian faith is unique	Christian Faith results in conflict	The church will result in tension with other faiths.	Problem Solving	Christianity is unique and should not be mixed with other religions.
193.	Acts 22	Gospel a stumbling block to Jews	Gentiles	Some cannot believe the Gospel is for all	Memory	A large telephone book. God wants all to be saved, regardless of background.

#	The Text	Theme	Major Word or Concept	Sermon Theme or Idea	Outline Type	Objects
194.	Acts 23	Impure always accuse others of impurity	White washed wall	The church is always charged with impurity	Hard Saying	Anything filthy; half painted white, half not.
195.	Acts 24-26	In chains for the sake of the Gospel	Chains	Often the believer suffers much for the Gospel	Doing	Military medals compared with Baptismal Certificates as "medals."
196.	Acts 27	Even a shipwreck a chance to preach	Giving Thanks	All events are opportunities for spread of Gospel	Divergent	Examples of surprising situations where the Gospel has been effective.
197.	Acts 28	Paul finds greatest freedom in chains	Preaching	God's word spreads to the great city	Chronological	Example how a rough situation can be turned to good.

CHAPTER FOURTEEN

Sermons for Children
From the Revelation

The revelation to the Apostle John, or the Apocalypse as the Greek text has it, though known to countless millions of Christians, is perhaps the most difficult book in the scripture for the average reader to understand. This cryptic message to the early followers of Christ concerning the end times on earth has consistently baffled the intelligence of the world's greatest theologians for two thousand years. As such, this work must be included in a book on the sermon for children. Children are indeed capable of understanding the major concepts of the Revelation of St. John. After all, the book was written to be understood by the faithful.

This book called the Revelation is heavenly or eternal truth wrapped in earthly and limited language. Contained in the book are mention of the remarkable realities that unfold the eternal covenant of God with Israel by means of mundane and earth- centered words hardly fit to describe the truth. The Revelation tells what no ear has heard and exhibits for the faithful to see what no eye has seen. So God has chosen to describe the indescribable, to display what cannot be displayed, to reveal what before was unrevealable, to cause to be comprehended what is not comprehendible by mere mortals. The fact that the painting of the book of Revelation is so difficult for adults to interpret is no stumbling block or limitation for children since it has always been the job of children to interpret and understand the cryptic messages of adults -- they, therefore, can understand what God wants them to understand.

The author has chosen a traditional interpretation of the

book of Revelation, which simply means we understand what was meant literally in a literal sense and what was meant figuratively in a figurative sense. The substance of the Revelation is not to be found in elaborate schemes of interpretation but in an understanding of the symbolism of the Old Testament and the covenant with Israel. This view will not allow a strict chronological interpretation of the book, but understands the text more like a symphony where the theme is immediately established, several movements and variations on the theme are explored, and there is a triumphant return to the theme in the final movement, or climax or conclusion. Thus, what is to transpire in the latter days is discussed several times in the Revelation, but not necessarily in a strict time sequence.

The inevitable and glorious climax of the Revelation is the real substance of the vision to St. John. The undeserved covenant made by God will culminate in the glorious, eternal reign of His beloved Son, the King of Kings and the Lord of Lords whose kingdom shall never end. The earthly church, continuously buffeted about by evil each day of its existence, will be wonderfully and remarkably triumphant in the end and the heavenly church will flourish. All evil will be tossed into the depths of the sea like a heavy millstone never to appear again. What God has promised shall indeed come to pass. One day the full power and glory of God will be unleashed during the final harvest and the royal kingdom shall be established where all tears shall be wiped away forever. This children yearn for and this children can comprehend.

#	The Text	Theme	Major Word or Concept	Sermon Theme or Idea	Outline Type	Objects
198.	Rev 1:1-3	Future plan	Revelation	God knows all that is to happen	Chronological	A map with a battle plan.
199.	Rev 1:4-7	Joyful Living	Freed us	Forgiveness	Logical	A chain that stops you form moving. It protects you from danger.
200.	Rev 1:8	Alpha and Omega	Almighty	God has the power to accomplish anything	Convergent	Large cards with "A" to "Z" on them.
201.	Rev 1:12-16	The Lord described	Son of Man	Sword	Theological	A two edged blade; symbol of judgement.
202.	Rev 2:1-7	He holds the keys to hell	Key	The Lord controls all	Mystery	A large oversized key.

#	The Text	Theme	Major Word or Concept	Sermon Theme or Idea	Outline Type	Objects
203.	Rev 2:1-7	Church at Ephesus	Abandoned first love	Church must be pure in action as well as doctrine	Hard Saying	A copy of the church constitution.
204.	Rev 2:8-11	Church at Smyrna	Faithfulness	Faithfulness	Doing	A crown.
205.	Rev 2:12-17	Church at Pergamum	Manna	Doctrine must be pure	Nature	Uselessness of 50% salt & 50% sugar solution.
206.	Rev 2:18-29	Church at Thyatira	Deep things of Satan	Do not toy with evil things	Logical	Show how you can get stained just being close to a dangerous chemical..
207.	Rev 3:1-6	Church at Sardis	Spiritual slumber	Awake from spiritual slumber	Chronological	The Book of Life; alarm clock.

101

#	The Text	Theme	Major Word or Concept	Sermon Theme or Idea	Outline Type	Objects
208.	Rev 3:7-13	Church at Philadel-phia	Keep the Word	Reward for keeping the Word	Doing	A strong pillar, unmovable door or crown.
209.	Rev 3:14-22	Church at Laodicea	Indifference, lack of commitment	God requires commitment	Nature	Demonstrate the uselessness of lukewarm water.
210.	Rev 4:1-6	The Rainbow of Heaven	Sign of the Covenant	The Covenant is a central feature in the Presence of God	Nature	Rainbow - cross reference the story of Noah.
211.	Rev 4:6-11	God is the center	Holiness	God remains holy always	Music	The hymn "Holy, Holy, Holy."
212.	Rev 5	Lion of Judah worthy	Lamb	Jesus is worthy of worship	Nature	Emphasis on US. A globe where the universality of redemption can be shown.

#	The Text	Theme	Major Word or Concept	Sermon Theme or Idea	Outline Type	Objects
213.	Rev 6:9-11	Waiting for the Day of the Lord	Martyrdom	God will wait for the full number of martyrs	Word Study	Written reports of martyrdom for the Lord.
214.	Rev. 6:12-17	The Day of the Lord	Day of Wrath	The Great Day of the Lord	Hard Saying	A scroll that can be rolled up quickly.
215.	Rev 7:1-8	Servants of the Lord saved first	Seal	Believers will escape tribulation of last day	Logical	A seal that shows legal ownership.
216.	Rev 7:9-17	Countless number saved	Great white host	God will save more than we expect	Nature	Bucket filled with sand. Reference covenant promise to Abraham.
217.	Rev 8-10	Plagues on the earth	Bitterness	Judgement on the unbeliever is bitter for believer	Nature	Something that looks good to eat, but that is bitter.

103

#	The Text	Theme	Major Word or Concept	Sermon Theme or Idea	Outline Type	Objects
218.	Rev 11	Covenant in force until the last day	Covenant	In the latter days the Covenant still in force	Chronological	Model of the Ark of the Covenant.
219.	Rev 12	War in Heaven	The Accuser thrown down	Satan cast out	Textual	Examples of charges and specification in a trial. These are thrown out because of the Lord.
220.	Rev 14	The wicked will be trod in the grape press	Justice of God	The wicked shall be destroyed	Hard Saying	Either a coffee grinder or grapes that are crushed.
221.	Rev 16:12-17	Readiness	Day of the Lord	Readiness for the Lord	Mystery	Alarm clock.

#	The Text	Theme	Major Word or Concept	Sermon Theme or Idea	Outline Type	Objects
222.	Rev 18:21-24	End of the wicked	Millstone	The wicked utterly destroyed	Nature	A heavy stone that will sink.
223.	Rev 19:1-8	Righteous deeds of the Saints	White purity	Deeds of the righteous not forgotten	Memory	Beautiful white linen.
224.	Rev 19:9-10	Happiness of Believers	Invitation	God will invite you	Theological	Samples of Marriage invitations. Invitation to banquet.
225.	Rev 19:11-21	Judging with Fire	Lake of Fire	The Believer will escape the fires	Nature	Any demonstration that shows the destructiveness of fire.
226.	Rev 20:11-15	The Book of Life	Book	Is your name in the Book of Life?	Convergent	A large book or Register. A parish register.

#	The Text	Theme	Major Word or Concept	Sermon Theme or Idea	Outline Type	Objects
227.	Rev 21:1-4	Renewal	New heaven and earth	God will make all things new	Chronological	Example of a famous building torn down and reconstructed to be more glorious.
228.	Rev. 21:5-8	Reward of Believers	Inheritance	An inheritance awaits you	Word Study	Examples of a will. God's is perfect.
229.	Rev 21:9-21	The City of God	The Radiance of the Eternal City	the glorious city God has prepared for you	Hard Saying	Compare a handful of nails and bolts with a handful of colored glass resembling jewels.
230.	Rev 21:22-27	Perfect liberty in Heaven	Open Gate	Wonderful life in Heaven	Logical	Use an open door.
231.	Rev 22:1-5	Tree of Life	Tree of Life	The Garden of Eden regained	Textual	Abundant food and water for the wayfarer.

106

#	The Text	Theme	Major Word or Concept	Sermon Theme or Idea	Outline Type	Objects
232.	Rev 22:16-17	Invitation	Come	God's invitation to all is the same	Theological	Flash card with word "Come" on it.

CHAPTER FIFTEEN

Sermons for Children From Romans and Hebrews

One of the chief concerns of parents and religious leaders in our modern society is that children receive sufficient doctrinal instruction to resist the evil and negative teachings to be found in a culturally failing society and community. Biblical knowledge is low and doctrinal ignorance is high in the community at large today as far as adults are concerned. Evidence for this is seen in the alarming success of "far out" religious sects and cults which previously were not able to interest mainstream Americans. Children are in need of basic Christian doctrine as never before since so many opposing viewpoints seek to be heard. What is needed is clear biblical teaching that is unchanging and easily understood by children.

The two New Testament books best able to teach this basic Christian faith and doctrine are Romans and Hebrews, both of which were written for the purpose of transmitting the doctrine of the Christian faith to new believers. Children are new believers, too! Romans was written to the recent gentile convert and Hebrews to the convert from Judaism who had some understanding of the Old Testament and the covenant.

All great Christian theologians have found the substance of the faith clearly delineated in the book of Romans. It has been said that no other book is needed in order to teach the entire Christian faith to anyone. Each article of faith is discussed thoroughly. Romans is nothing less than a handbook of the Christian faith.

The book of Hebrews is also a doctrinal handbook, though

its theme is more restricted in a Christological sense, dwelling more on the nature and work of Jesus Christ, His relationship to the Old Testament covenant, His offices as Prophet, Priest, and King. Nonetheless, a careful study of this book reveals its great doctrinal scope which is certainly suitable for children.

In this section there is a marked difference in the sense that the terminology of the faith needs to be taught as well as the content. Children should become familiar with the basic theological vocabulary that is to be heard and used during a lifetime. Objects in such sermons for children should be examples of how theological concepts exist but should not obscure the actual terms themselves which must also be learned. In other words, the theological term and concept exist together and neither should be emphasized at the expense of the other so that children actually grasp both.

#	The Text	Theme	Major Word or Concept	Sermon Theme or Idea	Outline Type	Objects
233.	Rom 1:1-7	Gospel	Gospel	Good news for all	Television	Article from paper of major interest or television.
234.	Rom 1:6	Chosen	Called	Called to belong	Riddle	Feeling that results from being called or singled out in a crowd.
235.	Rom 1:7	Chosen	Saints	The true nature of Saints	Chronological	Just as tools are made for special purposes, so saints are set apart for special service to God.
236.	Rom 1:11-12	Spiritual gifts	Charismata	Spiritual gifts are to be used	Doing	A wrapped Christmas package that has not been opened or used.
237.	Rom 1:16-17	Gospel	Power	The Gospel is the Power or dynamite of God	Problem Solving	Use rocks as symbol of the hard soul of man & dynamite which breaks it apart, revealing the inward part.

110

#	The Text	Theme	Major Word or Concept	Sermon Theme or Idea	Outline Type	Objects
238.	Rom 1:17	Being Right with God	Faith	True faith brings righteousness	Logical	Have a blind folded child stand on two boxes; have the child jump off into your arms. Faith is the trust the child had that you would catch her. Righteousness is the reward of faith, living in the presence of God.
239.	Rom 1:18-23	The Wrath of God	Without excuse	Man's great sin	Theological	Any example where people know something but refuse to live accordingly and are hurt thereby. This demonstrates man's one great sin & the fact that he is without excuse before God.
240.	Rom 1:24	To be Changed	Exchanged	Man exchanged godliness for ungodliness	Word Study	Show foolishness of choosing a picture of $100 bill instead of the bill itself; explain what each could do or mean.

#	The Text	Theme	Major Word or Concept	Sermon Theme or Idea	Outline Type	Objects
241.	Rom 1:28-32	Spiritual death	Filled	Mankind is filled with sin which is proof of his separation from God	Color	Label a container "Man". Select several base descriptions of evil and fill up the container to show man's evil nature separated from God.
242.	Rom 2:1-11	Good and evil acts	Impartiality	There are only 2 possible wages for mankind and God is impartial in payment	Memory	Two different paychecks describing the wages mentioned in the text.
243.	Rom 2:12-16	Doing is necessary	Hearing is not enough	Hearing God's word is in itself not enough	Doing (Action)	People can hear the warning that the dam is going to break; unless they do something right away they will be drowned.
244.	Rom 2:17-29	True religion a matter of the heart	Circumcision a matter of the heart	To God the inward is more important than the outward	Logical	No matter how good you are at guessing you never know what the inside of that watermelon is like until you see the inward part. Man is like this.

112

#	The Text	Theme	Major Word or Concept	Sermon Theme or Idea	Outline Type	Objects
245.	Rom 3:1-8	God is Faithful	Faithfulness	God is ever faithful, ever sure	Parent	Demonstrate how people make promises but can't keep them - God keeps his.
246.	Rom 3:19-26	Purchase of mankind	Redemption	Bought back by God	Chronological	People are like POW's captured by the enemy. The redemption price was God's own Son, the Redeemer.
247.	Rom 3:25	Jesus as expiation	Expiation	Jesus covers the law for us	Hard Sayings	Use A-V methods to show Ark of the Covenant with mercy seat that covers the law.
248.	Rom 4:1-7	Counting	Counted	Something for nothing	Mystery	A check book with balances. Jesus adds to our balance as a free gift. We had no balance in our account - now we do.

#	The Text	Theme	Major Word or Concept	Sermon Theme or Idea	Outline Type	Objects
249.	Rom 5:1-5	Christ died for us	Weakness	Saved while helpless	Convergent	Picture of helpless baby. God saved us while we were weak sinners. Baptism of children.
250.	Rom 5:18	Disobed-ience/ Obed-ience	Obedience	The results of obedience given to us	Textual	Because of Christ our report card before God is excellent.
251.	Rom 6:1-8	Death-Life	Baptism	Baptism kills, gives life	Logical	Just like a seed must die to produce life, Baptism kills but gives life too.
252.	Rom 6:19-22	Eternal life as a gift	Gift	Life in Christ a free gift	God's Hard Sayings	Give a child a gift he did not expect with no strings attached.
253.	Rom 7:21-25	Prisoners of Sin	The Good	Sin always attaches itself to the good we do	Divergent	Use a dye to show that even good deeds can be tainted in the Christian's life on earth.

114

#	The Text	Theme	Major Word or Concept	Sermon Theme or Idea	Outline Type	Objects
254.	Rom 8:1-4	No judgement for those in Christ	Condemnation	Being in Christ protects us	Problem Solving	Use concept of old sewer line continuing to function with a new slip line.
255.	Rom 8:14-17	God's family	Sonship	We are heirs	Forever	Use a human will to discuss relationship of father to son.
256.	Rom 8:37-39	Conquering	Over conquering	The Love of Christ enables us to do more than necessary	Doing	Long lasting batteries outshine others because of their stored energy. The Christian is the same.
257.	Rom 9:15-18	Mercy	Compassion	Mercy & compassion are God's to give as He pleases	Nature	In our humanity, our compassion is restricted. God's is unlimited, like the stars in heaven.
258.	Rom 10:9-13	Condition for Salvation	Speak Confess	Unconditional Promise	Logical	Use conditional warranty compared to God's unconditional promise.

#	The Text	Theme	Major Word or Concept	Sermon Theme or Idea	Outline Type	Objects
259.	Rom 10:12	Salvation is for all	All	The promise is to all mankind	Hard Saying	Use examples of human exclusiveness as opposed to God's inclusiveness. The smallest word, <u>all</u> holds the greatest promise.
260.	Rom 10:21	Why are some not saved?	Hand that holds Life	God's hands remain open today	Textual	Hold desirable objects in open hands, inviting children to take them.
261.	Rom 11:16-17	The root gives life	Tap root, grafting	Jesus is the taproot of Faith and Life	Word Study	Use a plant with exposed, healthy roots.
262.	Rom 11:33-36	All good things are in Him	Plentitude (fullness)	In God is fullness of Joy	Music	Find musical score for this doxology and teach to audience.

#	The Text	Theme	Major Word or Concept	Sermon Theme or Idea	Outline Type	Objects
263.	Rom 12:1-3	Be changed	Meta-morphosis	Christians are transformed by Spirit	Chronological	An object that changes from dull to brilliant, ugly to beautiful.
264.	Rom 12:3-8	All believers have useful gifts	Measure of faith	Though gifts are different, we share benefits	Divergent	Example of orchestra though different instruments only one sound really.
265.	Rom 13:11-12	Be Ready- end at hand	Awakening	Be alert, each day we are closer to the end	Chronological	Alarm clock.
266.	Rom 14:12-20	Judging others	Judging	Judging others destroys the Work of God	God's Hard Saying	Make up a religious report card and show how detrimental it would be.

#	The Text	Theme	Major Word or Concept	Sermon Theme or Idea	Outline Type	Objects
267.	Rom 15:14-16	Filling	Overflow	God has power to overflow the believer with joy and peace	God's Forever Sermon	A container that can be overfilled and contents splashed out. Blessings flow forth.
268.	Rom 15:17	Glory in Christ Jesus	Glory	Our higher glory or Recognition comes in Christ	Chronological	Diplomas & degrees these fade. The glory of Christ remains forever, in and with the believer.
269.	HEB 1:1-2	God's Word to man	By His Son	The Word of Jesus is the Word of God	Theological	Various manmade modes of communication that can be misunderstood. In Christ there is no confusion.
270.	HEB 2:1-3	Stay close to the Word	Drifting	Stay close to the Word lest we drift away	Logical	A boat or land compass to show direction.

#	The Text	Theme	Major Word or Concept	Sermon Theme or Idea	Outline Type	Objects
271.	HEB 2:8-9	Christ tasted death for all men	Taste	We need not fear death for Christ already tasted it for us	Problem Solving	Parents taste bitter things first for children. So does Jesus.
272.	HEB 2:14-18	Jesus understands our temptations	Temptation	Because He was true man Jesus understands temptation today	Linear	Examples of temptation in children's lives. They are never alone.
273.	HEB 3:12-19	Unbelief leads to unrest; belief to rest	True Rest	When in Christ man can know rest	Theological	Compare good and bad sleep. The believer shall enter into God's good sleep. Sabbath Rest.
274.	HEB 4:14-16	Coming to God	High Priest	We are free to approach the Throne of God	Logical	Contrast earthly and heavenly High Priest.

119

#	The Text	Theme	Major Word or Concept	Sermon Theme or Idea	Outline Type	Objects
275.	HEB 5:1-5	High Priest	Calling	The High Priestly calling of Christ	Divergent	Use the Order for Ordination; how much greater is Christ's calling!
276.	HEB 5:11-14	Milk-Meat	Nourishment of milk	Seek the milk of God's word - Purity	Color	A coke bottle and a bottle of milk.
277.	HEB 6:9-12	Spriritual product-ivity	Laziness	The diligent Christian produces a crop like well-watered land	Logical	Contrast the results of laziness and diligence in the life of children by concrete example.
278.	HEB 7:11-23	Christ is a perfect priest-hood	Indestruc-tible	Christ is the indestructible high priest	Convergent	Use a stole to contrast the baseness of the earthly priest to the heavenly one.

120

#	The Text	Theme	Major Word or Concept	Sermon Theme or Idea	Outline Type	Objects
279.	HEB 7:26-28	Sacrifices	One Sacrifice	The one sacrifice of Christ is sufficient	Chronological	Compare/contrast temporary sacrifices of old covenant with one sacrifice of the new. Use sacrificial instruments.
280.	HEB 8:1-2	Taber-nacle	The true Tabernacle	The incomparable Tabernacle created by God	Forever	Pictures of churches that are no more.
281.	HEB 8:5-13	The new Covenant	Covenant	In the new Covenant Christ tabernacles with us	Problem Solving	The old tabernacle was transitory. The new one is eternal. Even the Great Pyramid continues to decay.
282.	HEB 9:1-9	Way to the Presence of God	Holy of Holies	Christ is the way to the Presence of God	Problem Solving	Picture or model of the Temple.

#	The Text	Theme	Major Word or Concept	Sermon Theme or Idea	Outline Type	Objects
283.	HEB 9:11-27	Inheritance	By His Death, Christ activates the inheritance	Because of Christ we are partakers of the Will God made	Logical	Show how a human will comes into effect. God's is now in effect.
284.	HEB 10:1-18	Christ the real sacrifice	Shadow	The old law a mere shadow, Christ's sacrifice worthy	Riddle	A shadow is only animation, not the real thing.
285.	HEB 10:19-25	Access to God	Holy of Holies	Access to God open for all believers	Forever	A model of the Israelite Temple.
286.	HEB 10:35-39	The reward of confidence	Confidence	Confidence can be lost - hold on!	Doing	A bicycle or other object that requires confidence to operate.

122

#	The Text	Theme	Major Word or Concept	Sermon Theme or Idea	Outline Type	Objects
287.	HEB 11	Saints of old wait upon us	Faith Completed	We will be made perfect with the Saints	Logical	A book that is only partially completed.
288.	HEB 12:1-12	The race of faith	Perservere to finish the race	Cast aside all that encumbers your race	Theological	Picture of olympic runner with hands up at finish line.
289.	HEB 13	Beware of strange teachings	False doctrines and requirements	Do not be carried away by false requirements	Linear	Examples of strange religious teachings or practices.
290.	HEB 13:20-21	God adjusts the faithful to be well pleasing	Adjustment	Let God do the adjusting	Problem Solving	An instrument that needs to be adjusted by an expert.

CHAPTER SIXTEEN

Sermons for Children
From the Good News
According to John

Of the gospels, the book of John speaks most directly to children, or to those new in the faith. Partly this is due to the chronological nature of the text. Additionally, the book is so popular because of the powerful figurative or picture language used to describe God's plan of salvation for mankind and the nature of His Son, Jesus Christ.

Within this gospel we have the figures of the door, the gate, the shepherd, the way, the truth, the lamb, the vine and branches, the light, hunger and thirst, the good shepherd, the feeding of five thousand, fish and bread, the woman caught in adultery, stoning, the calling forth of Lazarus, Jesus weeping, etc. The figures are full of meaning and power for people of every age and time. In a manner similar to the Revelation, the heavenly truths of God are here garbed in everyday picture language. The writer of the sermon for children is soon overwhelmed by the objects that can be used while preaching from the gospel of John.

As well, there is the grand scope of the story of salvation. This begins, we are told, before time began in the counsel of God: the Father, the Word, and the Spirit. The Word incarnates upon the earth as the Son of God sent to rescue mankind. Mankind, of course, does not want rescue, as evidenced by the powers that be, the Jewish leadership and the Roman government. At each turn of events, though, the power of God is displayed through the Son by means of the miracles or signs that speak directly to the people lost in sin. Inevitably, with purpose, Jesus lays down His life for the sins of the world. The empty tomb is the last and most powerful sign of the authority of Jesus, the now resurrected, glorified Word who returns in power to the Father. The absolute power of Christ is perceived in the forgiveness of Peter by the Lord, in contrast to the deceit and evil of the church leaders of the day. This risen Lord, this eternal Word, this Lamb, this Gate, this loving Shepherd, this Light of the world is worthy to be believed and worshipped until the glorious kingdom comes.

What God in eternity planned has come to pass. Eternal life is open to all. Death has been conquered, and in His presence there will be fullness of joy unspeakable.

This is the antidote for the child who fears the dark. This is the food for the boy or girl who is spiritually starving. There is a father for the child who is parent-less. There is someone who can lead the young person on the way of life. There is the water of life from which our children can drink and never thirst again. In Him, and only in Him, will they find fullness of joy. The gospel of John can bring all of this to the little ones the Savior calls His own.

#	The Text	Theme	Major Word or Concept	Sermon Theme or Idea	Outline Type	Objects
291.	JN 1:1-14	Word made flesh	Tabernacle	Jesus camped with us	Chronological	A tent
292.	JN 1:29-34	Sacrificial Lamb	Taking sin	Jesus takes our sins away	Theological	An eraser
293.	JN 2:1-11	Miracles reveal Christ's glory	Sign, miracle	The signs reveal the Authority of Jesus	Convergent	What signs reveal Jesus today?
294.	JN 2:12-24	Prophecy of Death and Resurrect-ion	Sign, miracle	The Resurrection is a sign of the Glory of Christ	Word Study	Metamorphosis - a chrysalis
295.	JN 3:1-15	Born from above	Re-birth	Baptism is from above, heavenly work	Textual	A Birth Certificate & Baptismal Certificate.

126

#	The Text	Theme	Major Word or Concept	Sermon Theme or Idea	Outline Type	Objects
296.	JN 3:16-21	God's over-whelming Love for Creation	Gave (Gift)	In Jesus, God gave us an unspeakable gift	Linear	A prized possession that can be given away.
297.	JN 3:19-21	Jesus is the Light of the World	Light	Jesus brings light to a darkened world	Forever	A darkened room represents the earth before Christ came.
298.	JN 3:31-36	The Anger of God	Wrath	Faith in Jesus removes the wrath of God	Riddle	A filter - God sees us through the filter of His Son.
399.	JN 4:1-13	Spiritual Thirst	Water of Life	Jesus provides what is essential for life	Memory	A glass of water
300.	JN 4:34-37	Harvest of Eternal Life	Eternal Life	Jesus announces the Great Harvest	Nature	Anything that has been harvested.

#	The Text	Theme	Major Word or Concept	Sermon Theme or Idea	Outline Type	Objects
301.	JN 4:39-42	Harvest of eternal life	Samaritans	Eternal life open to all	Hard Sayings	A members only sign - or any sign that excludes.
302.	JN 4:43-54	A miracle reveals Authority of Jesus	Sign	The works of Jesus prove who He is	Divergent	A Degree or professional license.
303.	JN 5:1-28	The work of God and Jesus is continuous	Work	While the world sleeps, God still works for the harvest	Logical	Idea of the farmer who harvests at night so we can eat during the day.
304.	JN 5:28-29	All the dead shall hear his voice	The Voice of Christ	The dead in Christ shall be called to life	Theological	The coffin as a resting place.

#	The Text	Theme	Major Word or Concept	Sermon Theme or Idea	Outline Type	Objects
305.	JN 6:1-14	Feeding of the 5,000	Feeding Sufficiency	Christ has power to feed us today	Doing	A basket of fruit - one but needs to take what is offered.
306.	JN 6:16-24	Jesus walks on water	Fear not	When Jesus is near, fear flees	Memory	Example of being alone and fearful, or with someone and safe.
307.	JN 6:25-35	Jesus is the unspoiled Bread of Life	Bread	Jesus is the Bread of Life	Mystery	Two pieces of bread; one pure the other spoiled.
308.	JN 6:35-37	In Christ, spiritual hunger evapor-ates	Hunger	Jesus is the Bread of Life	Nature	Loaf of bread - example of the filling that comes after the hunger.

#	The Text	Theme	Major Word or Concept	Sermon Theme or Idea	Outline Type	Objects
309.	JN 6:39	Jesus shall bring all believers to the Father	The Last Day	Jesus shall resurrect us Himself at the Last Day	Music	The hymn "A Hymn of Glory Let us Sing" epitomizes God's promise of resurrection.
310.	JN 6:44-59	The mystery of being with Christ	Body and Blood of Christ	Communion with Christ gives us eternal life	Mystery	The communion cup and plate.
311.	JN 8:1-11	Woman caught in adultery	Salvation is for all	No sin is too great to be forgiven	Music	The hymn "Chief us Sinners."
312.	JN 8:12-13	Walking in the Light	Darkness, Light	Jesus helps us walk in the Light	Problem Solving	Two flashlights; one with weak batteries, the other with strong.

#	The Text	Theme	Major Word or Concept	Sermon Theme or Idea	Outline Type	Objects
313.	JN 8:31-39	Freedom	Truth sets us free	Jesus tells the truth that makes us free	Word Study	Chains and a lock with key.
314.	JN 8:42-47	Deafness of unbelief	Hearing	The unbeliever hears but does not under-stand	Hard Sayings	Read a passage from Scripture in a foreign language.
315.	JN 8:48-58	Jesus claims Divinity	I Am	Jesus and the Father are One	Theological	Two placards with words "I Am" on them.
316.	JN 9:1-12	God often works through people	Display through spit and mud	God often displays Himself through human frailty	Chronological	Any example where God is glorified through human weakness.
317.	JN 9:13-34	Belief responds with Glory to God	Glory, Recognition	Faith glorifies the work of God and Jesus	Music	Folk hymn "Children of the Lord."

#	The Text	Theme	Major Word or Concept	Sermon Theme or Idea	Outline Type	Objects
318.	JN 10:1-10	Jesus is the gate to Life	Gate of the sheepfold	We can trust Jesus for entrance to the Kingdom	Riddle	Example of sheep. They wait for shepherd.
319.	JN 10:11-12	Jesus is the Good Shepherd	Good and bad shepherd	The sheep are protected by the Good Shepherd	Forever	A shepherd's staff or crook.
320.	JN 10:14-21	The Good Shepherd	Life as sacrificial	Jesus gives His life for the sheep	Nature	Picture of shepherd and sheep.
321.	JN 10:25-28	The Good Shepherd	Seize; snatch	No one can steal the sheep from the Shepherd	Forever	Picture of shepherd and sheep.
322.	JN 11:1-43	Jesus has power over death	Resurrection	If He can raise Lazarus, He can raise us	Logical	Anatomical diagram of human body. Why life is impossible after three days.

#	The Text	Theme	Major Word or Concept	Sermon Theme or Idea	Outline Type	Objects
323.	JN 11:25-26	Life without death	Resurrection	The Promise of Jesus	Music	Compare power of Promise of Christ with powerless-ness of people's promises. Hymn: "Jesus Shall Reign."
324.	JN 14:5-8	Jesus the Way	Road	Jesus knows the road to life, the way to the Father	Linear	A map for a journey. You must know the way.
325.	JN 15:1-17	Jesus the Good Vine	Bearing Fruit	Those in Christ bear good fruit	Textual	A bunch of excellent looking grapes.
326.	JN 19:17-24	Jesus dies on the Cross	Crucifixion	Jesus was crucified for the sins of the world	Divergent	A cross.
327.	JN 20:1-17	The Empty Tomb	Resurrection	Jesus is a resurrected Lord	Music	Hymn "Jesus Christ is Risen Today."

133

The Text	Theme	Major Word or Concept	Sermon Theme or Idea	Outline Type	Objects
#					
328. JN 20:19-23	Breath of Spirit	Holy Spirit	Jesus extends the power of forgiveness through the Holy Spirit	Chronological	Picture of dove - Peace that the Holy Spirit gives.
329. JN 20:24-31	Miracles	Signs	The miracles of Jesus bring us to faith	Music	Hymn "My Faith Looks Up to Thee."

CHAPTER SEVENTEEN

Conclusion

The task set before the Christian Church has never been complicated nor insurmountable. The entire substance of the directions to the church by the risen Lord can be summarized in a few words: GO AND TEACH AND BAPTIZE; FEED MY SHEEP; AND LOVE ONE ANOTHER EXACTLY AS I HAVE LOVED YOU. The church, however, through the ages, has often been engaged in matters altogether different. Where does the church of today discover the drive and power to accomplish the simple goals set forth by the Lord? The answer today is the same as it was two thousand years ago when the bewildered disciples stood gawking at the Lord rising up into the heavenly cloud. The answer is found in the short but cosmic promises the Lord connected to the commands: ALL AUTHORITY HAS BEEN GIVEN TO ME IN HEAVEN AND ON EARTH, and LO, I AM WITH YOU TO THE CLOSE OF THE AGE.

The task of the church leader, in part, is the feeding of the little sheep in the fold. The desire of the Lord is that not one be lost, not even one. May the sermons for children we prepare transmit the love of Christ to His little ones now and to eternity!

BIOGRAPHY

Paul M. Adams is an ordained clergyman in the Lutheran church. He has held membership in the Lutheran Church - Missouri Synod, the Association of Evangelical Lutheran Churches, and the Evangelical Lutheran Church in America.

He holds the Bachelor of Science degree in Education from Concordia Teachers College, Seward, Nebraska; the Master of Divinity degree from Concordia Theological Seminary, Springfield, Illinois; the Master of Science degree in Educational Administration from Nova University, Ft. Lauderdale, Florida; and the Doctor of Ministry in Theology Degree in Church Growth Studies from Fuller Graduate School of Theology in Pasadena, California.

Dr. Adams helped to establish a campus ministry at Arizona State University for his denomination. He served three years as a missionary and formed new congregations at Prescott Valley and Black Canyon City, Arizona. He used Church Growth principles to revitalize an inner city church in South Gate, California and initiated a cross - cultural ministry there. He has taught for the University of Nevada. More recently he has helped to form a new mission congregation in Elko, Nevada.

The author now lives in northeastern Nevada, teaches middle school and junior high school students, and writes and publishes articles and books as an avocation.